UP!

The Difference Between
Today and Tomorrow Is You

BY BOB RAVENER

UP!
The Difference Between Today and Tomorrow Is You

By Bob Ravener

Praise for
UP! The Difference Between Today and Tomorrow Is You

Through sharing stories of his own personal background and experiences, Bob Ravener gives us the insight and tools to achieve our goals. Bob shows us that life's opportunities are to be embraced with enthusiasm and perseverance. In doing so, success will surely follow.

~Eric Foss
CEO, Aramark, Inc

Bob tells a powerful story that everyone can share in. The perseverance he has shown in his journey is inspiring—a benefit to us all.

~Joe Gibbs
Owner, Joe Gibbs Racing
Former Head Coach of the Washington Redskins

As a military officer, I recognize the critical leadership skills and traits that Bob Ravener highlights throughout *UP*. His courage to publicly discuss his upbringing and to draw life lessons from adversity are the reasons that this book should be mandatory reading for training future leaders in any organization. He captures the essence of earned success.

~Terry M. "Max" Haston, Major General USA
Adjutant General, Tennessee National Guard

UP is an inspiring and valuable book for anyone who is struggling to stay afloat in these turbulent times. I work with thousands of job seekers all over the US, and some of the biggest obstacles they face are feelings of hopelessness, despair, and lack of confidence about their future. Bob's true-life story about overcoming adversity and achieving his dreams in the face of overwhelming odds, is sure to give hope to many people. It's a great story, and the happy ending is one that we all can aspire to achieve for ourselves. Bob Ravener is the teacher, the inspiration, the friend that we all need at some point in our lives.

~Steven J. Greenberg
Host, CBS Radio News *Your Next Job*, Founder, Jobs 4.0

This book is a must read for every leader's journey. Bob Ravener inspires us to take heart, chart a path, and embrace opportunities against all odds in our lives and work.

~Mark C. Thompson
NY Times Bestselling Author & Executive Coach

Thirty years ago, I was 27 years old, 160 lbs, and last played football when I was 21. My lifelong dream was to play in the NFL and score a touchdown for the winning Super Bowl team. The obstacles I faced were enormous, and I was told it was an almost impossible task. One great book that helped inspire me to realize my dream was *The Power of Positive Thinking* by Dr. Norman Vincent Peale. *UP* is a modern day how-to book that adds a very personal account of overcoming life's hurdles and attaining success on many levels. I knew Bob at the Naval Academy, and my memories were that of a bright young man with a sunny disposition. I had no idea of the dysfunctional family issues he had to deal with just to get to the Naval Academy. Not only does he tell a story of family pain that is all too familiar to many of us, he offers step-by-step solutions to conquer everything that got in his way. This book is a must read for those who dream of success but feel they can't get there. Bob and I did it, and so can you!

~Phil McConkey
Super Bowl Champion with NY Giants and
US Navy Veteran

Bob Ravener's practical, common sense approach to high achievement comes from hard, real-world experiences and an unparalleled determination to excel. The lessons and, more importantly, the path forward he advocates, can inspire all who wish to find the best that is within them or seek to overcome hardship and obstacles in their lives.

~Dan Lyons
Graduate of US Naval Academy and Oxford University, 1988 US Olympian and Founder of Team Concepts, Inc.

UP! The Difference Between Today and Tomorrow Is You—a primer to success. Bob Ravener's example of how he confronted, coped with, and adapted to his abusive alcoholic father, and how he realized he had to take charge of his life, which he did, was instrumental in laying a strong foundation upon which he built the walls of his life. His drive and determination, coupled with his motivation to succeed, set the course. He channeled his athletic ability and leadership in student activities to improve his self-esteem and self-confidence. His time at the USNA was the launching pad to the success he attained in the corporate world. He should be known as "The Great Juggler" since he set his priorities, mastered time management, set his goals, and never said I can't, it's too hard, or I can't find the time. He never considered failure as he "juggled" corporate responsibilities, family, furthering his education, volunteerism, coaching, and his personal physical fitness regime. Bob's ability to navigate the challenges of his personal and professional life—to do the right thing, at the right time, for the right reason—reveals a man who not only remained faithful to his God, his family, and his fellow man, but a man who put a plan in motion to make the most of every day, and made it so. I am proud of his accomplishments and grateful to be able to call him my friend.

~H. C. "Barney" Barnum, Colonel of Marines (Ret)
Medal of Honor Recipient

Bob has written a book from the heart, one that will help anyone that spends time with it. Bob's story is truly inspiring, a tough march from a challenged childhood to the heights of corporate America. It, however, is much more than that—it is instructive. He guides us to reflect on our own lives for the lessons that are embedded in our own experiences and personal trials. Bob teaches us that success requires not only perseverance but also thoughtful reflection on the direction one should take.

~Ron Porter
Vice Chairman, CT Partners

The author's life story validates the important role America's military plays in developing the leaders of our nation's civic and business life. He tells it all: his story is compelling, and the fact that he had such a difficult young life is heart wrenching. But the retelling of it reveals a determination and resilience that nearly every one requires to be successful and happy today. *UP! The Difference Between Today and Tomorrow Is You* will be instructive to anyone, younger or older, who hopes (but doesn't believe) that a difficult beginning isn't going to doom them. It offers concrete life-planning tips and guidelines that will instruct younger readers and will cause older readers to say, "Yes, he's nailed it. A life well lived is one you work hard for."

~Leslye A. Arsht
Former Deputy Under Secretary of Defense for Military Community and Family Policy

Yes, good things do happen to good people. But make no mistake—that outcome is neither random nor accidental. Although faith or fate or karma may play a part, Ravener's story shows us that fulfillment—personal and professional—is mostly about hard work, commitment, self-knowledge, resiliency, character, personal responsibility, and relationships. At times gut wrenching, at times humorous, *UP! The Difference Between Today and Tomorrow Is You* is more than a heartfelt, touching, inspirational, and bittersweet memoir. It is also a textbook for success. In fact, it should be required reading for anyone who signs up for that course called *life*.

~**Tom Wolfe**
Career Coach, Author, Columnist, & Veteran

I have known Bob since his arrival at Dollar General in 2008. The most amazing aspect of my relationship with Bob is that, until reading this book, I had no idea of the hardship he had encountered growing up. You see, somewhere along the way, Bob made the decision to build the life he wanted and not the one given to him during his childhood. Bob is one of the most determined, focused, and cheerful executives I work with. His transformation is somewhat analogous to the transformation he and the rest of the management team executed at Dollar General. Bob's book, *UP*, is a real-life story that is guaranteed to inspire you to get up and get going—build the life you deserve.

~**Mike Calbert**
Member & Head of Retail Industry Team, KKR

Motivational! A must read for anyone looking to improve their outlook on life. Bob Ravener shares the experiences that challenged and inspired him to develop the character and leadership skills which directly translated into a highly successful career and life.

~**Dale Nees**
Assistant Dean, Mendoza College of Business,
University of Notre Dame.
Former submarine commanding officer,
Captain, U.S. Navy (Ret)

UP: THE DIFFERENCE BETWEEN TODAY AND
TOMORROW IS YOU!, BOB RAVENER

Published by Lighthouse Publishing of the Carolinas

2333 Barton Oaks Dr., Raleigh, NC, 27614

ISBN 978-1-938499-70-8

Copyright © 2013 by Bob Ravener

Cover design by Wisdom House Book: www.
wisdomhousebooks.com

Available in print from your local bookstore, online, or from
the publisher at: www.lighthousepublishingofthecarolinas.com

Library of Congress Cataloging-in-Publication Data

Bob, Ravener.

UP: The Difference Between Today and Tomorrow Is You! /
Bob Ravener 1st ed.

Printed in the United States of America

Lighthouse Publishing
of the Carolinas

www.lighthousepublishingofthecarolinas.com

Table of Contents

$\mathcal{D}$edication

This book is dedicated to all those who saw in me hope,

who gave of themselves for my growth,

who sacrificed much to give.

I will never forget!

An Extraordinary Journey

We've all read books about individuals who have overcome considerable odds to succeed. Sometimes conquering those odds leads to personal growth or gain, and sometimes it leads to professional accomplishments. Rarely, as you read those books, do you find that the journey results in both, and rarely can you say that you actually know the individual who "conquered the odds." Bob Ravener's journey has indeed led to tremendous success and fulfillment, both in his personal life as a husband, father, and friend and in his professional life as a successful human resources executive and leader in a Fortune 200 company.

I have known him for only a short time, but Bob is one of those individuals you feel you have known forever. Quite honestly, after reading this remarkable book, I wish I had. Bob's story is an example of "iron will" over and against a set of circumstances that would overwhelm most people, and it could easily have led to tragedy instead of triumph.

Bob's life began in a family atmosphere of abuse, alcoholism, and constant disruption as he and his family moved from one place to another. His childhood was characterized by uncertainty, misery, and crushing poverty. Yet he managed to find enough glimmers of hope, and of a better world, to suggest that maybe he could fight his way out of the abyss. His unwillingness to allow his circumstances to define either him or his future translated to hard work in school and athletics. It also took him to the US Naval Academy and a starting position on the Academy's baseball team. But his challenges were not over, and we discover in these pages how he, over and over again, fought back and ultimately prevailed, though sometimes in unexpected ways.

Bob learned that we are only as big as our dreams, that failure is just an opportunity, and that anybody we meet, any day, under any circumstance, may provide the inspiration we need to take that next step. Those inspirational people, some of them children, taught Bob invaluable lessons: how to trust when he had been unable to do so, how to believe in others when he had always been skeptical in the past, and how to invest unselfishly in others even though many in his life had been unwilling to invest in him. Bob learned that we gain the most in giving back, and he has given back by assembling his own life lessons and passing them along to others through coaching, counseling, and, now, through this book.

Bob learned most of those lessons the hard way. Now he believes in himself and in what he is capable of accomplishing. He knows that values are shaped, good and bad, by the company we keep, that the dreams we choose must have obstacles or they are not really dreams, and that disappointments are nothing more than a necessary part of a meaningful life journey.

Watching Bob's approach to his career, his family, and his commitments, and his always-positive attitude has taught me more than all of the classrooms and self-help books I have encountered. I know you'll learn similar lessons as you read his story. Bob's extraordinary journey, overcoming the barriers he has faced along the way, proves that the inner soul can indeed conquer all.

Rick Dreiling
Chairman and CEO, Dollar General Corporation

A Common Dream

I have often reflected on my life, how I arrived where I am, living the American dream. Many people haven't ended up in the same place, and what's worse, they won't—either because they've stopped dreaming or because they simply don't have the right keys to the right doors. I'm not talking about success or about how I, and many of my associates, have achieved it. More important than either of those subjects is how others can achieve it too.

I don't see myself as anything extraordinary—no Albert Einstein or Lee Iacocca, no Martin Luther King, Jr. or Franklin Roosevelt, or anyone else who has left a legacy of greatness. Nor do I profess to be an expert on the topic of success, like Stephen Covey, for example. These individuals, and others like them, have reason to be household names. I, on the other hand, am much more similar to all those who will never be celebrities yet are surrounded by talent—if you look in the right place. In fact, I have worked with and for some of the brightest and most talented people, people who have been and always will be extremely successful. All of them have achieved great things, but only a few had to maneuver the kind of roadblocks I have encountered.

Most of us, about 99.9 percent, never will be famous. Fame isn't the point. The point is that millions of people, between the time they wake up and the time they go to sleep at night, experience a living hell, or at least a life that falls far short of their own expectations. How can someone overcome that kind of adversity, accomplish something in their own life, and make a difference in the lives of others?

What I have learned from others, what has worked for me, has also benefited many others before me. You may already be doing much, if not all, of what I describe. However, just like a car needs to run on all cylinders to perform at peak levels, you can't master only a part of what's in this book and hope to succeed. You need to use the broad spectrum of suggestions. Only then can you begin to realize your potential fully—personally, professionally, or both. That has been the key for me. For a long time I succeeded in one or a few of these areas. It wasn't until I started to develop a wider array of traits that my own positive steps began to multiply.

This book offers insights, based on my real and often tenuous experiences, to those who are trying to improve their happiness quotient by reaching their full potential. It all begins with a belief in yourself and the willingness to take a step forward.

Many people have aided me along the way, and I'll introduce you to them. I also believe that the USA is still the land of opportunity if you know where to look and how to get there. As much as anything else, this book is a tribute both to those who have given of themselves to me and to this nation I love so dearly.

Everyone's path and the circumstances that propel them down that path are unique. I hope that my life experiences and the simple yet challenging lessons I have shared in this book will make your journey smoother. Chasing the dream, taking a risk, believing in yourself, and giving back to society along with perseverance, attitude, values, and focus—these lessons are meaningful and useful for everyone who dreams of success.

Let the journey begin.

Bob Ravener
Executive Vice President and Chief People Officer,
Dollar General Corporation

THE *Summit*

A Panoramic View

You can't build a reputation on what you're going to do.
~ Henry Ford

On August 20, 2009, 4:00 p.m. (CDT), I sat in the executive conference room, also known as the "Think Tank," at Dollar General Corporation's headquarters outside of Nashville, Tennessee. Seated around the thirteen-foot rectangular conference table with me were four other senior executives, including the CEO. The silence was palpable. We had all been anticipating this moment for several months.

That afternoon we wrestled with a significant decision that had implications across the entire business community. We pored over the latest drafts of legal documents deemed necessary to form a new board of directors. But we were all very much distracted, waiting for the call we expected at any moment. Once or twice I caught myself staring at the exotic Anigre wood-paneled walls or rubbing my thumb across the high gloss lacquered finish of the table.

We knew what we hoped we could shortly tell the employees—that the company was filing an application with the Securities and Exchange Commission to once again become a publicly traded company. KKR, the renowned private equity firm, had purchased Dollar General Corporation in 2007. Their own business model projects a five-year holding period for the management team to turn a company around and deliver sufficient profitability to take it back into the public arena.

Dollar General had accomplished the turnaround in less than half that time.

As the clock ticked past 4:10, I glanced at Susan Lanigan, the highly capable top company lawyer, better known as the general counsel. We had planned to gather all the company leaders in the boardroom once the filing was confirmed, but they didn't know our intentions yet, and the clock ticked ever closer to the New York deadline. Everyone fidgeted, drumming fingers on the table, checking BlackBerries, shuffling papers—anything but mentioning what was upmost in our minds.

At 4:12 Susan checked her BlackBerry for about the twentieth time in the last ten minutes. Suddenly she leaped up in her chair and proclaimed, "It's filed!"

The rest of us jumped up from our seats, slapping high-fives all around. Rick Dreiling, the down-to-earth, motivational CEO, headed for his office. David Tehle, the no-nonsense, meticulous numbers guy and CFO, raised his eyebrows and grinned from ear to ear. Susan clutched her BlackBerry as though loosening her grip might negate the news we had just received. Christine Connolly, the corporate secretary, remained focused and intent. She was already flipping through the legal encyclopedia she stored in her brain.

The pre-arranged message went out to the company leaders: meet with Rick at 4:45.

Thirty minutes later, in a packed room on the fourth floor, and with many more people listening via phone, Rick stood at the head of the room, took a deep breath, and congratulated his colleagues and employees. All their hard work over the last eighteen months, since the company had been taken private, had paid off. Dollar General was taking the first official step forward.

As I stood next to Rick, observing the satisfaction on the employees' faces, a surge of pride swept through me. To be part of this event and the executive team, to play a role in helping the company arrive at that momentous occasion—I felt like we had just won the seventh game of the World Series.

KKR had purchased Dollar General for more than $7 billion. At the time, lending markets had just begun to experience some downward pressure, a trend that quickly accelerated over the following months. The country rapidly descended into a deep recession that perilously teetered on the collapse of the US financial markets in late 2008 and early 2009. By June of 2009, the unemployment rate was running at 9.5 percent, the highest level in more than twenty-five years, and business grappled with an overall negative economy that by some estimates had cut more than three million jobs in the previous eighteen months alone.

To have a stable business during those tumultuous times, much less to continue to grow—to add thousands of jobs rather than eliminate them—was a tremendous accomplishment. Newspapers across the country headlined layoffs, foreclosed homes, shuttered businesses, and wrecked lives. The country had sunk into the "Great Recession," reportedly the worst economic crisis in the country since the Great Depression of the 1930s.

For Dollar General to be at that point in the turnaround after only two years—and more astoundingly, after Rick had taken the helm only eighteen months before—was as hard as it gets in the business world for a complex company. Dollar General was already among the largest companies in the country with more than 8,000 stores and over 80,000 employees spread across thirty-five states. In fact, it had performed so well that everyone involved in the planning was confident that investors would buy up the stock once it hit the New York Stock Exchange's trading floor. Truly an amazing feat by any standard, exceeding everyone's expectations by a wide margin.

But it had been a long journey for me to get to that point in my life—proud, excited, fulfilled—at the pinnacle of my career. I absorbed the exuberance in the room, the enormity of the moment. The sweat equity, innovative ideas, and flawless business execution had paid off. I smiled broadly, lifted my head, and gazed out the window. In the distance the Tennessee hills stood tall and strong. So did I.

GET *Up!*

Early Lessons

In the middle of difficulty lies opportunity.
~Albert Einstein

I first realized something was wrong about my family in the winter of 1964 when the world I knew was snatched from me. During the first five years of my life, our family lived in a modest split-level home that backed up to a boat marina. Seagulls squawked incessantly. On many days the distinct smell of freshly brushed varnish and the gritty sound of boat owners sanding their vessels filled the air. On hot summer nights, the foul aroma of dead fish, clamshells, and sea grass wafted through our windows.

I wrestled with my brother in the playroom downstairs, studied the world through the front windows that overlooked Main Street, and watched *The Lone Ranger* and *The Little Rascals* on a small black and white TV. Normal kid stuff. A few fond memories stand out: a family trip to the 1964 World's Fair in Flushing Meadow, my grandfather bringing a freshly baked crumb cake when he visited, and a glimpse of someone I thought was Santa Claus standing under a streetlight on a snowy Christmas Eve.

Then my father's business folded. We moved from the house my father had built in Long Island, New York, to a cramped house across town. It was the first of many moves from one house to another, transferring from one school to the next, like we were gypsies staying one step ahead of trouble. I was a kindergartner, and the trauma of facing a new set of classmates halfway through the year unnerved me.

More disturbing, though, was my abusive father who took his anger out on me and my older brother, Tom— most of it landing in Tom's lap. Picture a home in which peace ruled only when the father was absent. When he did come home, he seemed to be a man possessed by evil spirits—a horror I later realized was the life-altering effect of alcoholic binges. I sought refuge at friends' houses, school, and, early in my life, with my mother. She provided a safety zone, at least for me.

Early on, Tom took out his frustration with my father on me. Fifteen months my senior, he was big enough to routinely beat me up, pick on me, and further isolate me in front of his friends when he wanted to show who was in charge—as older brothers often do. Tom and I had both inherited the blue eyes and fair skin of my mother's Irish/ German ancestry and none of the physical traits of our Italian heritage. We both sported the popular crew cuts, dark blue jeans, and sneakers, known as PF Flyers, of the sixties.

Since Tom was older, taller, and more gregarious than I was, I tried to match him in every activity. I asked to play ball with Tom and his friends. Invariably I was picked last—or, as the odd man out, never picked at all. Many times, banished to the sidelines, I watched the others have fun and compete while I fantasized about my heroes, the Yankees, with the likes of Mickey Mantle, Bobby Richardson, Whitey Ford, Clete Boyer, and Elston Howard—stars of the championship teams the Yankees fielded year in and year out. Bobby Richardson became my favorite for no other reason than we had the same first name. Often I went home crying because the older kids made fun of me.

My mother spent hours throwing a ball to me in the

backyard, or at least it seemed that way to me. She was tall, about five foot seven, and thin—majestic, in my eyes. She tossed the ball to me underhand, first at short distances, then moved progressively farther away. Like most six-year-olds, I dropped the ball more times than I caught it at first. Those backyard tosses stand tall in my memory. I don't recall my father ever having a catch with me, ever interacting with me like that.

I idolized my brother. Being rejected by him and his friends crushed me. In an effort to be liked by his friends, I suppose, Tom chimed in when the older kids made fun of me, all too often joining the chorus of verbal taunts that highlighted my lack of strength, coordination, and ability to match up to the skill level of boys two or three years older than I. On the few occasions when I was able to play—because there was nobody else to round out a team—the chorus of laughter grew worse when I struck out or missed a ball in the field. Kids can be cruel like that.

Tom and I fought and jawed back and forth with one another. My mother often referred to us as Cain and Abel, those biblical brothers whose inability to get along ultimately led to Abel's death at his brother's own hands. We were too young to recognize that the wedge between us was directly linked to our abusive father.

The rejection I encountered early in life spawned an inner fire and strength to succeed when least expected. The experience also taught me that I had to take ownership of my improvement if I was ever going to get into the "game." On the playgrounds of New York, our fields were often made of concrete and asphalt. I used the side wall of the school, chalk to draw a strike zone, and a beloved pink Spaulding rubber ball to throw against the brick wall. The rhythmic pop and bounce of the ball against the wall steadied me, satisfied me—almost like a riff playing over and over in my head. I learned the value of practice and routine.

Stickball and stoop ball were staples during that era for any youngster with dreams of wearing Yankee pinstripes. So I decided not to watch anymore. Refusing to be humiliated again, I didn't show up for any of my brother's games for quite some time. I was determined to show him and his friends that I could compete, so I played side-wall ball instead. *My* game was the imaginary Yankees against the other New York team, the expansion Mets, whom traditionalists of the game hated at the time. Having memorized their lineups and stats from watching the games on TV and trading baseball cards, I played countless games with myself and kept track of the team records from my one-on-one encounters.

Eventually I added a friend, and two-player stickball and stoop ball became a real competition, one that fueled the fire inside me, not to mention dramatically improving my hand-eye coordination. Standing ten feet away from a stoop and having a bouncing rubber ball repeatedly coming back to me at a high rate of speed and at different angles definitely improved my reflexes.

Accurate aim was crucial in stoop ball. The player had to hit one sweet spot on the three-stair brick-faced stoop for the ball to rebound into his hands instead of caroming off into the yard or down the street. Large trees lined the curb, creating perpetual shade and an uneven playing field. Their roots had long ago pushed up the sidewalk. I ended up with quite a few scraped knees, stumbling over the uneven terrain as I chased an errant "fly ball." All the more challenging. All the more fun.

Even today, common professional reaction and

coordination drills use the same principles to improve reflexes. When I got back into the game with my brother and his friends about a year later, I was able, thanks to my intense practice and growth spurts, to compete at their level, though I still had not reached Tom's level of ability. My commitment to compete with my brother and his friends built my confidence and helped me realize for the first time that working harder than others at something could make a measurable difference.

Moving became commonplace for our family. It seemed we were always off to another town. Sometimes I played with the boxes, making forts, hideouts, or campsites. But moving also meant another round of proving myself—a new school, new playmates. When I turned eight, I finally competed in organized ball, playing my first Little League season in Malverne, New York. A key recollection of that season is the absence of my parents at most games, a lingering scar that has not faded with time.

In hindsight their absence at my games was a good thing since my father berated Tom during his baseball games. I vividly recall Dad standing behind the backstop at Whelan Field in Malverne. The baseball diamond was positioned between a main road and a small river. The babble of the water and the scent of fresh cut grass were always marred by my father's relentless criticism of Tom's every move.

Tom, the catcher, was always within ten feet of my father's voice. It seemed like Tom couldn't do anything right. I watched his frustration and anger build throughout the game. For the most part, he weathered the verbal barrage with dignity. He blocked the barbs aimed at his character and skill almost as masterfully as he blocked errant pitches in the dirt. Somehow he managed to be a strong, tough player—as if being a catcher was something he was born to do.

Why the coaches never intervened is beyond my comprehension. Maybe they spoke to my father privately and he just ignored them. It wouldn't surprise me if he had. His stubbornness, magnified by alcohol, made him both hardheaded and cold-hearted.

For me, though, the field of play generated real passion, even though I endured the extreme disappointment of losing the league championship and failing to make the all-star team at the end of my first season in organized sports. Like most boys, I thought I was better than I really was, even though I provided solid support for the team as a hitter, pitcher, and fielder. That athletic failure was my second scuffle with rejection. And while it was a small setback, probably unnoticed by anyone other than me, it became an inner challenge. Would it lead to a lifelong pattern of failure and rejection? Or would I take the pain and will it in another direction, one that would be a positive force for change? I chose to work at it, moved up to the "minor leagues" the next year, and made my first all-star team. The trophy I received is the only one I kept over the years—a reminder of what it takes to excel.

Sparks Fly

For all of our difficulties, I ended up in what I considered better environments than my brother did. And in spite of the struggles our family endured, my mother at least had the wherewithal, if not the finances, to keep us out of the "projects"—the common New York term for the ghetto or low-income housing, where far greater challenges were a daily part of life. Unfortunately, the decent roofs over our heads came at the expense of everything else necessary to give a child a head start on a better life.

Schools are a perfect example. Maybe Tom needed the structure that Catholic schools afforded. He excelled there. I enjoyed it too. One day, however, my first grade teacher asked me to deliver a note to the teacher in Tom's third grade class. When I arrived, the teacher, a nun, teased me with a wooden paddle. "I use this on students who misbehave," she said. "I hope you're not one of them." Fear gripped me. A few tense moments passed. Not until the class broke out into giggles did I realize she was joking. What a relief!

When we moved for the fourth time, Tom, a fifth grader, had to attend a large district middle school, where he no longer received as much individual attention. I benefited from the nurturing environment of the local elementary school for three years, still innocent enough to avoid many of the social pitfalls of the day.

Both public schools were racially mixed, complete with challenging politics of the sixties, but I developed some strong relationships. Racial tension was uncommon in my elementary school, primarily, I suspect, because our young minds had not yet been poisoned by the world around us. There was some name-calling and a few other minor incidents, but nothing severe. The junior high and high schools, however, were another story. Those students contended with overcrowding along with the usual adolescent peer pressure and brash cockiness. Combined with the racial overtones of the day, the schools were proverbial accidents waiting to happen. Tensions ran high between the black students and white students. Racial slurs were slung back and forth not only among students, but even more so among adults.

In 1967, the country was trudging awkwardly and painfully through the Civil Rights Movement. The Vietnam War also marched quickly toward greater unpopularity. Both the movement and the war generated national unrest, especially on college campuses. On one hand Dr. Martin Luther King, Jr. preached nonviolence; on the other hand, the Black Panthers and militant antiwar activists believed the best path for change came through force. By the time 1968 rolled around, the country ticked toward explosion like a homemade bomb.

My brother and I viewed life from different angles. Neither of us was much interested in what was going on in the world, but we couldn't escape Walter Cronkite on the six o'clock news. Each night graphic film footage flickered across our black and white TV screen: soldiers in yet another firefight, carrying stretchers of wounded comrades in a faraway place; a protest march in a distant US city; President Johnson's grave face mouthing somber words about other conflicts, more deaths.

Just in 1968 alone, a series of events rocked the country. Johnson announced he wouldn't seek reelection as president. Dr. King and Bobby Kennedy were both assassinated within nearly two months of each other. College students marched violently in cities and on campuses, most notably at Berkeley and Columbia. The Tet Offensive and My Lai Massacre aroused great anguish over the war. Two black US athletes, Tommie Smith and John Carlos, punctuated the frustration of black Americans by raising their fists over their heads while "The Star-Spangled Banner" played during the medal ceremony at the Mexico City Olympics. Their controversial act signified their unity with other black Americans, but it also defied what they believed to be a repressive US government. Violent protests blistered the Democratic National Convention in Chicago. Finally, the close and controversial election of Richard Nixon to the White House closed out one of the most violent and volcanic years in our nation's history, ultimately forcing seismic shifts in the political and social landscape of our country.

I was in the third and fourth grades during 1968, Tom in the fifth and sixth. He began to depart from his usual jovial demeanor to one of an angrier, less careful person. Part of it was the constant barrage of criticism from my father, perhaps driving Tom either to prove himself even more or else to give up on succeeding at all since he would never live up to Dad's expectations. The other dynamic was the beginning of adolescence and a desire to fit in among his friends if he couldn't please his father.

Whatever the psychology, it was a formula for disaster. As Tom's grades eroded, Dad's criticism intensified. As the verbal whippings accumulated, Tom's will to succeed on the traditional level evaporated. Although I was somewhat aware of the strife plaguing the American landscape, Tom immersed himself in it. He was already a rebel, and while the school focused on calming the waters, Tom wanted to stir them up. The middle school tensions ran high as he and his fellow students looked out their classroom window, which faced the high school across the street. They watched the protests and fights erupt between racially divided students while the establishment, symbolized by black and white police cars, was called to the scene on several occasions in an effort to quell the swirling unrest.

Natural Integration

One volatile issue that divided the nation was forced integration in public schools. Many black students were bussed to my school, located across town from a predominantly black section called Lakeview.

All of us inevitably come across people in life we quickly erase from our memory. Then others, often for inexplicable reasons and maybe even in brief encounters, create an indelible mark in our minds. Solomon Titus was one of those individuals for me.

I befriended Solomon, a young African-American kid, when I was in the fourth grade. My white friends and I walked what seemed like miles to school through the lily-white part of town. In reality it was only half a mile. When Solomon had to walk, he hiked more than twice that distance from his home in the predominantly black Lakeview section of Malverne—including a long hike through the white section. In retrospect, he was courageous to make that walk along the symmetrical streets lined with the modest homes and well-kept lawns. He also bravely befriended me, apparently not caring how others felt about it.

On the few occasions I walked with Solomon down Lakeview's streets, I never saw another white face. Not that I expected to see one. From what I knew of the world, I assumed the races just lived in separate neighborhoods.

Our paths didn't cross every day because we each had our neighborhood circle of friends. But when we did walk side by side, there were never any racial overtones. Just two friends laughing and joking on the way home from school.

I can't place my finger on why Solomon and I became

friends, but a bond developed that was as strong as it was brief. Solomon was smart and I liked talking to him. He was also tall and lanky yet quite strong. I was just an average-sized kid—about four feet tall, fifty pounds. During recess, we boys played pickup football. The game had one object: the ball carrier had to make it to the schoolyard fence before someone, or a gang of someones, tackled him.

Solomon became my protector. Not surprisingly, disagreements and sometimes shoving matches broke out among the young males during the game. A kid would say that he was tackled too hard or someone had stolen the ball from him. If I was involved in the pushing match, Solomon rushed to my defense. He commanded the respect of not only his black peers but the white kids as well. His combination of physical strength, brains, and finesse enabled him to talk through situations without resorting to physical violence.

Even while walking with me through the white part of town, Solomon showed no sign of uneasiness. His happy-go-lucky mentality indicated that nothing was going to bother him. I relished our discussions about baseball, schoolwork, or virtually any other topic—other than race. Bullies had sometimes chased me and my other friends when we walked home, but when I walked with Solomon I felt no fear. I observed and tried to emulate his calming, confident swagger.

Adult tensions and general uneasiness between white and black students surrounded me. But my relationship with Solomon seemed natural. I realized, even then, that the color of our skin had nothing to do with friendship. Genuine concern and some common interests solidified our rapport. That lesson took root in my heart; it has produced fruit throughout my life.

Although my friendship with Solomon was an asset in my young life, I had many liabilities stacked up against me—none more intense and devastating than my father's alcoholism.

Reflection Questions

1. Bob acknowledges that he is the product of an unstable and dysfunctional family. What would you identify as the greatest asset of your family background? What would you identify as the greatest liability?

2. Bob recalls that his older brother Tom took the brunt of his father's abuse, and then took out his own frustrations on Bob. How can you relate to Tom? How can you relate to Bob?

3. When Bob felt insecure as a child, he escaped into an imaginary world of playing baseball for the New York Yankees. What kind of escape mechanisms did you employ when you were a child? How about now?

4. A painful memory that has lingered throughout Bob's life is the absence of his parents at his Little League games. How much did your parents support you in sports and/or other activities? How has that affected you?

5. Who has been your "Solomon Titus"—a person of another race or vastly different background whose friendship has helped you cross significant boundaries?

Darkest Before Dawn

Learning is not child's play;
we cannot learn without pain.
~Aristotle

As I matured, I became more aware that my circumstances were far from normal. By the time I was eight years old, my family had already lived in three different houses in two different towns. My brother and I had attended four different schools and we barely saw our father. When he was around, tension filled the air. I had also realized that the place my father liked best was any pub he could find. He had his favorites, of course, but any place that sold alcohol suited him just fine.

Trying to generate the fatherly love I craved, I accompanied him on his "errands." More often than not, I sat at a table near the bar with several soft drinks, always topped with cherries. Long before mobile devices and video games existed, all I had to pass the time were my natural senses. In a strange way, I relished the surrounding aromas and noises generated by the frantic activity in the establishments—clanking glasses, silverware, and animated conversations (although the collective white noise made it impossible to decipher any one particular interaction). Smiling faces, bellicose laughter, and backslapping at the bar created a false notion that all was well in the world. Large fans slowly circulated overhead, spreading the sour smell of spilled alcohol, which seeped into everything, including my skin and hair.

When I wasn't drifting into a daydream of some

sort, my eyes scanned the room. I studied the ceiling tiles, particularly impressed by ornate tin ceilings laced with intricate designs and patterns. The soundless TV hovered above the bar, its annoying horizontal lines constantly running down the screen since picture quality was poor in most places. Cobwebs in the ceiling corners invariably swayed in the light air, making me fantasize about haunted houses or some other creepy adventure. Sometimes I counted the number of bottles behind the bar or the tiles and wood slats in the floor.

My father seemed so important because anytime we walked into one of those places he was greeted with cheers and backslaps. Little did I know his "fan club" was just his drinking buddies, always three sheets to the wind and, like Dad, mostly unemployed. As they hunched over the bar, their backs blended into a composite, nameless wall.

When I did glimpse their faces, the men all looked the same to me: a few days of facial hair growth, uncombed hair, red spider veins on their faces and noses, large, calloused hands and muscular arms that looked like they had worked hard for a long time. My father seemed to think it was a sign of strength, dignity, and his stellar character to introduce me to the drunkards as his namesake. I can still feel the tight grips and hard edges of their palms as they engulfed my little hand.

I was always anxious to leave yet glued to my chair by my desire to be with my father. Sometimes I sneaked over to the shuffleboard game in the bar and spent what seemed like hours working on the right technique that sent the shiny silver discs skating across the wooden, sawdust-laden alley. Occasionally, I asked Dad if we could leave. But the longer he sat on the barstool, the less tolerant of me he became. One swat on the back of my head silenced me, and I shuffled back to my seat in the corner of the bar while my father continued to solve the world's problems with his buddies. Their boisterous voices and uncontrolled laughter drowned out any spark of rational conversation. They didn't allow one another to finish a thought or acknowledge that an opinion, different from their own, had merit. It was always a test of who could shout down the others and emerge on top. Today it is called the alpha dog syndrome, yet I never witnessed anything good emerging out of their raucous, testosterone-charged verbal bouts.

Why didn't I just stop going with him? Maybe I always held out hope that the next time I accompanied him he would take me somewhere special: the ice cream parlor, a movie, a ball game, or the park. Or maybe I thought my presence might prevent him from staying away from home for too long. Maybe if he left the bar sooner, he would be civil to my mother and four siblings, three of them much younger than I.

Occasionally, Dad was sober, and I yearned to duplicate those days. I clung to the faintest glimmer of hope that at some point there would be fun in my family again—like the family trip we had taken to the World's Fair back in 1964. In my mind, heaven was filled with the rides, displays, and shows I had seen that day.

Only once did Dad take me to his job site, which happened to be the highway construction on Long Island. That morning I tried to match his work clothes—canvas utility pants and boots. All I could find was a pair of old Levis with patches on both knees and my PF Flyers. My heart raced when I saw all the large machinery, especially the giant yellow earthmovers, their wheels taller than my dad—something I had read about in books but had never seen in real life. I watched in wonder as they worked in unison like a well-conducted orchestra.

Dad and I climbed up on a number of those massive machines. Riding in their cabs, as they performed their monumental work with the utmost precision, I felt larger than life. Dad allowed me to place my hands on the controls; I pretended to guide the giant's every move.

At lunchtime I sat by my dad—just one of the guys. Most of the men had the old-fashioned lunch boxes, containing hero sandwiches piled high with roast beef, salami, bologna, or ham. With dust from the roadwork swirling around us and tickling my throat, I almost choked on my Welch's grape jelly sandwich, but I managed to wash it down with a quarter-pint carton of milk. Being both close to my father and in the real world was exhilarating— if only for a day.

Yes, I cherished that experience. Yet my joy shattered when we stopped at the local watering hole on the way home. My father transformed into Mr. Hyde again. It seemed like more time passed in the bar than at the worksite as I watched my father drink a shot with a beer chaser, one after another, quickly succumbing to the alcohol high, making louder and more expressive gestures with each swallow. The laughter and voices grew louder after sunset. We finally left for home well after dark.

On the drive home (no seat belts back then), I feared for my life. Even to an eight-year-old, it was obvious my dad was inebriated. I closed my eyes to block out his reckless driving. I tried to pray the fear away, asking God to spare me from our impending death. When I tried to think about something far away, Dad brought me back to reality with a slap on the back of my head. Then he would rant about some foul attribute of my mother or Tom, or he would boast about how he was going to make it "real big" someday.

But he was my father. So as much as I wanted to hate him, as much as I wanted him to stop drinking, I looked into his bloodshot, puffy eyes and saw a love for me that I needed. One moment he shouted like a madman capable of the most heinous actions. The next moment he grinned and reminded me that I was named after him for a reason—that I would make him proud.

How does an eight-year-old deal with that? The only way I could. When he opened the front door at home, I ran up the stairs to the sanctuary of my room while my mother blasted him for keeping me out until all hours. She was relentless. Then he joined the fray, and the yelling and screaming continued into the wee hours of the morning. Finally, the effects of the alcohol silenced him—the barbs and venom ceased and he eventually passed out. I usually cried myself to sleep, the pillow over my head to shut out their hateful attacks. Nothing, however, provided enough protection from the sharp, stabbing words that stole a part of my childhood with each thrust.

Why? Because I wanted us to be a real family.

Those nights frightened me. I really believed someone was going to get killed. Then what would happen to me? The uncontrolled environment scared me, but the possibility of being left alone terrified me. Probably like a lot of kids, I "protected" myself by surrounding my bed with pillows and checking under the bed to ensure nothing was there.

I never went to work with my dad again, but I hoped that going other places with him would help. Trips to the market for a loaf of bread, to the store to buy me a baseball glove, or a routine ride to practice occasionally provided short periods of sober, coherent, and meaningful discussion with Dad. But much more frequent were bouts of incoherent, slurred speech produced by a stop at the closest "watering hole." Nothing I did helped. In fact, those futile efforts generated a deep-rooted fear of authority figures and a craving to belong, issues that stalked me for decades.

When my parents had pushed each other to the breaking point during those nighttime bouts, my mother sometimes pulled carving knives out of the kitchen drawer and lunged at my dad. More times than not, Tom or I stepped in to break it up. Occasionally, we ended up facing the wrong end of the blade.

I never heard my mother or father speak a kind word about or to each other. We children became sounding boards for their loathing of one another. My mother reminded us over and over again what a mistake she made by marrying our father and ignoring her father, who had been right about Dad. My father harped on how my grandparents pampered our mother and complained that she never had to live in the real world like he did. The decibel level and vitriol of their criticism increased with each swallow of alcohol.

Inevitably, my father's drinking problem led to financial problems. We were forced to move for the fourth time while I was in fourth grade. With no job and little money, my mother moved us in with her aging parents. My grandfather was a noble Army veteran, who enlisted as a private and retired as a colonel. He served during three wars and then patrolled the streets of New York as a cop during the Roaring Twenties and the depression-era thirties. He had little regard or tolerance for my father. Obviously, the situation was tenuous at best.

New Surroundings

My father wasn't living with us at the time because my
grandfather wouldn't allow him to enter the house. In fact,
I don't remember seeing Dad for months—not until he
picked us up at my grandparents' house one morning after
the school year ended and moved our family again.

Grandpa drove Tom and me across two towns every
day so Tom could finish sixth grade and I could finish
fourth grade in Malverne. I woke up at the crack of dawn,
dressed, and sat with Grandpa at the breakfast table that
my grandmother had prepared the previous evening. Each
morning, he removed his stubble with an old Remington
electric shaver, guiding its movement with a big round
mirror he stored in a cabinet behind the table. The sharp
click of the blades locking into place and the high-pitched
humming of the gears provided a soothing start to my day.
After he finished, he took out the blades and let me "shave"
as well. Then Grandpa ate a big bowl of wheat germ, a
banana, and some toast. Tea was his morning drink, and
I always felt older when he let me have just what he was
eating. His early morning routine modeled the art of
preparation and what it leads to—tranquility, confidence,
and levelheaded thinking.

Every morning the oval table was covered with a lace-
edged tablecloth, every place setting neatly laid out with
fine patterned bowls on top of plates, next to teacups and
saucers. Alongside the dishes, my grandmother placed
heirloom silverware and cloth napkins folded restaurant-
style. The scene is engraved in my memory mostly because
those few months were some of the happiest days of my
life, despite the difficulty caused by two families living

under the same roof. My parents didn't fight, my military hero grandfather spun tales whenever I asked, and a general feeling of security pervaded the house.

Initially, just Grandpa and I shared those mornings. Quiet, peaceful, and wonderful. Sometimes he asked me about schoolwork, other times about my activities, but always followed his questions with a lesson. He talked often about the reward of hard work and commitment. "Failing to do your best," he said, "should never be a reason for falling short of your goals." He always seemed to be in command of himself. No wonder his neighbors called him "The Colonel." He garnered respect not because he was a harsh man but because he cared about the world around him—including his grandkids. I always felt like I was at my best during those early morning routines. I realized that preparing in advance and sticking to a routine, like my grandfather did, had a lot to do with removing unnecessary stress and feeling ready for the day.

After breakfast Tom and I climbed into Grandpa's car, a 1948 Pontiac—the kind often used in old gangster movies. I pretended I was driving by imagining the large circular logo on the glove compartment was a steering wheel. Grandpa gave me a dollar for lunch. I ate at the five-and-dime store across the street from the school, having just enough money to buy a greasy burger, fries, and a drink. If I had an extra dime, I treated myself to a stick of licorice or some gum. At the end of the day, I walked to the public bus stop and met Tom there. We rode the bus from Malverne to East Rockaway, then walked a mile back to my grandparents' house. That afterschool trip was just another way I had to grow up faster than most kids. And boy, was I proud the first time I made the trek!

In June of that year, Dad followed through on yet

another get-rich-quick scheme. The whole family piled into an old Mercury station wagon with the faded wood grain on the side and paraded up to Connecticut to stay with my father's parents, who were also older, retired, and—until we showed up—happy.

Family Extensions

I never felt as close to my father's parents as I did to my mother's parents, maybe because my grandfather retired and moved from New York to Connecticut before I was born. Other aspects that distanced us, I'm sure, were their own stoic upbringing, their disappointment in my father, and the fact that they were older than my other grandparents.

My father's mother had been a US Marine during World War I. In fact, she was one of the first 305 women who entered the Corps when the Secretary of the Navy authorized women to serve in August of 1918. She joined a month later and served on both active and reserve duty for four years. Clearly the matriarch of the family, her toughness made it easy to believe she had been a Marine, a flinty warrior whose discharge papers were signed by the most famous Marine of all, General John A. LeJeune. My grandmother, Mary Coan Reilly, was all of five feet tall. Thin as a rail, she used a cane to compensate for a limp. She adorned her square face with fashionable eyeglasses. She had flaming red hair when she was young, but it was snow white when we lived with her. With Irish blood and Marine grooming, she didn't take any backtalk from anybody. She was quick to point her cane at someone; it didn't matter who they were. Sometimes she told my father off, saying she should wash his mouth out with soap, like she did when he was a child, because of his foul language. He swiftly changed his attitude in her presence—a sign of his deep-rooted respect for her.

My grandparents had retired to the "country" after living first in Brooklyn and then on Long Island, where my father grew up. Grandpa had been a career employee with Grace Lines in New York, working as a longshoreman on the docks as a timekeeper. My dad didn't seem to have much respect for him because of my grandfather's perceived "status" in life, though he did acknowledge that his father had been one heck of a pitcher. A lefty like me, according to one story he was going to a tryout with the Yankees when a bicycle accident ruined his arm.

My grandfather struck me as a hard-working, reliable man, with strong opinions about everything. I longed for the same kind of warmth I had received from my mother's father, but I never received it. Something very deep-seated bothered him. I don't remember him smiling or being patient around us, at least not in those cramped quarters. He always seemed pre-occupied. His patriotism, however, impressed me. Every day he raised and lowered "Old Glory" like clockwork on the flagpole he had erected in the front yard. In Connecticut, he ran the Ball Pond beach and served as a volunteer fireman. I admired his grit but, unfortunately, he never allowed me to get close enough to know more about him. Certainly part of his gruffness was brought on by my alcoholic father and by a family of seven, with little money and a lot of mouths to feed, living in his four-room house.

Add a troubled son and his family to a household of two decent people and disaster is unavoidable. I wondered if life could ever breed happiness. At the same time, I began to realize that it was up to me to climb out of that hole. I certainly wasn't getting help from my surroundings. I was determined not to be another casualty in the struggle between the grim survival and the unnerving insanity etched on my parents' faces.

Our short stay soon turned into a war of attrition. My father's problems intensified since we were forced to adapt to yet another unfamiliar environment in a confined setting. My younger brother, Greg, and two younger sisters, Danielle and Diann, were jammed into one of the bedrooms with my parents. Tom and I spent two long, miserable years sleeping on nylon cots in the middle of the living room while my grandfather religiously watched New York's channel 5 every night. I learned to loathe the nightly lineup of David Frost, Merv Griffin, and the ten o'clock news. Before the news started, the announcer always said, "It's 10 p.m. Do you know where your children are?" My grandparents absolutely knew—they had a front row seat! Little did it matter that two kids were trying to get a good night's sleep to be ready for the rigors of school and other activities.

Needless to say, I fell asleep around eleven o'clock or later, depending on what time my father came home from a night of drinking. Sometimes he wouldn't come inside at all. The next morning, I would find him passed out in his car—more than once oddly parked halfway off the driveway, with a dent or scratch from yet another brush with tragedy.

Circumstances compelled me to galvanize my emotions or lose my mind in the process. I pressed myself to compartmentalize the daily challenges of life so I could function in other areas and keep my eyes on the future prize: free myself from that miserable existence.

Testosterone Unleashed

About this time, Tom turned the corner on adolescence.
Some of the guys he was running with didn't graduate
from high school, and some ultimately ended up in jail.
This caused even more strain on the family, as fairly typical
adolescent behavior quickly shattered any hope that our
lives could ever be tranquil. My father took the brunt of
his own failings out on Tom, resulting in a chasm of hate
so wide that it became irreparable. At twelve going on
twenty, Tom was growing ever closer to my father's height
of five feet eight. They became two strong-willed warriors,
each trying to crush the other. And, unfortunately, their
war unfolded before the family.

One ho-hum summer evening Tom had been hanging
out with his buddies on the front lawn of one of their
houses. Smoking cigarettes and looking for mischief, he
and his friends must have done something to provoke Dad
as he passed by. When Dad pulled up in my grandfather's
car, the odor of sour liquor slammed into my face the
minute he opened the car door. He immediately began
ranting about the "zeroes" hanging out on the hill with
nowhere to go but down. Once inside the house, he
chastised my mother for not doing something about
her son. He kept ranting. As usual, my grandparents
tried to ignore their son—my grandmother prepared
dinner and my grandfather sat in his easy chair, hands
interlocked behind his head, watching a Mets game on TV.
Meanwhile, my mother turned the argument back on my
father and began criticizing him for his own failed dreams
and fantasies. I knew it was not going to be a good night.

As if on cue, Tom walked into the house with a tough-guy swagger. No sooner did he enter the room than Dad started pelting him with abusive language. Having endured it for years and finally feeling like he could do something about it, Tom dished it back. They got in each other's face, both red from the rush of adrenaline. Tom shook his finger at Dad. Drunk, but not about to be humiliated by a twelve-year-old, Dad smacked Tom across the face and told him to shut up. Tom laughed, shrugged it off, and said it didn't hurt. Then he taunted Dad, saying something like, "Oh, you think you're tough, but you're nothing but a drunk." Dad hit him again and Tom laughed again, which so enraged my father that he closed his fists and took a swing. Tom then lunged at Dad, not to hit him but to tackle him and prevent him from taking another swing. My grandfather rose from his chair, rushed across the room, and stood near them, trying to stop the melee. He instantly got knocked into the wall from the force of Tom's tackle.

All hell broke loose at that point as my mother, grandmother, and I scurried to break it up and tend to my grandfather. Luckily, he was not seriously injured, but that wasn't the best situation for a man over eighty to be in. That evening's battle ended, but the damage had been done. After that incident my grandfather wanted no part of us. And who could blame him? The unfortunate effects of alcoholism and abuse had claimed two more victims—my grandparents. The circle of destruction widened.

Ten years old and acting much like the second son, I was driven deeper into a fear of authority. You couldn't blame Tom, for he had seen the worst of my father's rage for years. Rebellion was inevitable. My father badgered him relentlessly and continuously called him a failure. On many occasions in one of his drunken rages, my dad predicted that Tom would end up in a prison cell. Slurring his words, he delivered his gruesome edict: "Eight by ten, Tom, you'll end up in a room eight by ten." Even then I cringed at the thought of a father burdening his twelve-year-old son with that kind of life sentence.

At the same time, I was thrust into the dual roles of developing child and pseudo parent—calm and conscientious on the outside, trying to keep my family intact—but torn apart on the inside, worried about how we would make it through the next day and wondering what would become of us all in the future. I steeled my resolve to work as hard as I could, absorb as much as my limited worldview would accommodate, and fight like hell to escape my destructive and debilitating home life.

My father's alcoholic slide into oblivion deeply affected us all, scarring my mother, my siblings, and me in immeasurable ways. I knew that my survival depended on my ability to climb the massive mountain of despair and deprivation that towered over me.

Reflection Questions

1. Bob fondly remembers the one time that he went to work with his dad. Do you have recollections of being with one or both of your parents while they were working?

2. Bob's most predominant memories, unfortunately, are of sitting off to the side while his father drank with his barroom buddies—and then of his parents fighting when he and his dad got home. Can you relate to those kinds of memories in some way?

3. Bob described his relationship with both sets of grandparents. How would you characterize your relationship with your grandparents?

4. Due to past struggles or problems, how prone are you to having a victim mentality? What would it mean for you to fight to get out of that rut?

Scale the Mountain

Though no one can go back and make a brand new start, anyone can start from now and make a brand new ending.
~ attributed to Marcus Aurelius

Arguably, no person in recorded history is more renowned for perseverance than Abraham Lincoln. Until he won the presidency in 1860, his life was a series of setbacks and disappointments. Even after that improbable triumph, he was constantly faced with great challenges both in his personal life and in his public life. Between 1831 and 1860, Lincoln was involved in a failed business and defeated in multiple elections for public office. He also lost a sweetheart to illness and had a nervous breakdown. Two of his four children died before he did. While President, he faced a hostile Congress, sometimes without the support of his cabinet. Though he faced many Union defeats in the first years of the Civil War, Lincoln remained resolute and committed to saving the nation.

Though I didn't recognize it at the time, perseverance was stamped into my makeup when I was a young boy. I saw what my father was doing to my brother and wanted to avoid his wrath at all costs. During those years I felt like Brutus, who betrayed his friend Julius Caesar. Attempting to endear myself to my father, I never sided with Tom. In fact, I distanced myself from him, hoping to avoid his fate. He, on the other hand, seemed to resent me for not sharing the brunt of our father's rage.

Still, an indestructible bond existed between us. Maybe

being thrust into another new environment and battling our father's wrath forged a foxhole camaraderie that nothing could sever. Tom and I attended the same school for three years. We were also teammates on a Pop Warner football squad and several baseball teams. Emblematic of his grit, Tom always played the tough positions—a catcher in baseball and a lineman in football. In the town's first Pop Warner football season, he even won the Most Outstanding Lineman award. He embodied the toughness I admired, but also avoided—it reminded me too much of Dad's wrath.

Consequently, Tom and I constantly struggled to close the wide chasm that developed between us over the years. Team sports helped to some extent. Even now our relationship only scratches the surface. Although we have made strides to move beyond the grim past, the visits are too few and far between. In retrospect, the pain was so great that I did everything possible to separate myself from it, to hide from the agony. It may haunt me the rest of my life.

To survive during those years, I focused on school and athletics, where my perseverance generated attention from others—positive attention that I sorely wanted and needed—first in Little League baseball, then in Pop Warner football, and finally in middle school basketball. I realized I had some talent, and I thoroughly enjoyed the competition. Participating in sports, a great energy release, also helped me forget about my miserable home life. In school, teachers warmed up to me. I responded with a desire to please them, pleasing myself in the process. Being at school, where all my friends were and where I could feel safe, was another release for me.

But my inner emotions had reached dangerous levels.

Embarrassed by my father's behavior and the life we were forced to lead, I refused to talk about my feelings with anyone. When I first began to play sports, he occasionally came to practice. Sometimes he could barely stand up. He yelled out slurred phrases that quickly scattered anyone within earshot of his voice. I immediately recognized the unmistakable nasal tone and looked in vain for a place to hide—on a baseball field, there is nothing but wide, open space and small blades of grass. If it had been possible, I would have crawled under the field.

Sometimes art really does imitate life. The drunken father played by Dennis Hopper in *Hoosiers* reminds me quite a bit of Dad although no happy, productive relationship between my father and me emerged— something Hollywood fabricates so well.

I often left class, ducked into the boys' bathroom, and cried in one of the stalls. I had no other outlet, nowhere else to turn. Somehow I managed to channel enough positive energy to stay on course, even if I was steering blind most days. One time I even walked out of class when a teacher confronted me for not paying attention. That demonstrated how close I was coming to losing it. Thankfully my football coach, John Zinser, happened to be walking the halls and guided me back to the classroom. No harm done.

But what about the next time? Something had to change before I snapped, but even then I recognized that some positive forces surrounded me. Although I never spoke about my family situation, people couldn't have been oblivious to it. Soon I noticed that others were looking out for me.

Our family lived in six different houses over a nine-year period, but at least we stayed in the same town, New

Fairfield, Connecticut, so I enjoyed the same activities, friends, and schools. Though I knew that other people were worse off than I was, we were impoverished both financially and emotionally. Sometimes we slept next to the fireplace for warmth because our power had been shut off. I loathed the indignity of asking the school lunch coordinator for a free lunch card so I could eat a nutritious meal. My mother didn't have enough money to keep us fed well, and what little we had was swallowed up by alcohol on a daily basis.

Many kids recall family vacations, shopping trips, or eating ice cream with their parents. We stopped at the supermarket to purchase two six packs of Schmidt's sixteen-ounce bottled beer for my father—*every single night*. My siblings and I each received one pair of shoes a year, usually at Easter. A highlight for Tom and me was a trip with our grandfather to the local Thom McAn shoe store in Lynbrook, New York. There we were fitted for what my grandfather knew to be quality shoes. The trip was timely as Tom and I often had to put cardboard inside our old shoes as protection from the elements; otherwise, the holes in the worn soles allowed dirt, stones, and rain to soil or soak our socks and feet.

Visiting my grandparents was our only family outing. Sometimes my grandfather took Tom and me to a park in East Rockaway that contained two World War II cannons. While we climbed all over those cannons, Grandpa highlighted the virtues of those two ironclad defenders of freedom and spun tales of his war exploits. Those occasions probably fueled my eventual intrigue with the military and American history.

My father's drinking alienated everyone we knew; consequently, our family was never invited to any social gatherings. I was fifteen before I ever set foot outside my home states of New York and Connecticut, saw a professional baseball game, or stayed in a hotel. Even then, I only went as far south as Philadelphia and never visited my beloved Yankee Stadium until much later in life. My godfather, Dick Orefice, afforded me these brief experiences that helped me understand there was a better world out there—which, in essence, changed my life.

In the interim, though, I excelled in both athletics and academics. Fortunately for me, a new high school had just been completed in New Fairfield. Since Tom was two years ahead of me in school, he was bussed to the next town, Danbury, where he was swallowed up in a large school that lacked the compassion, motivation, and resources to smooth the transition of kids coming in from another town. So in addition to missing another opportunity to stand out, attending yet another school forced Tom into another alien environment, which quickly disenfranchised him. Once again, he was an outsider, surrounded by a host of unfamiliar kids who, for the most part, had grown up with each other and stuck together.

An Awakening

On the other hand, high school was an awakening for me. Even though I had adapted to the town and environment over the previous four years, I entered a whole new world the first day of my freshman year, not just a new high school. It didn't matter that it was still partly unfinished. In fact, only the classrooms and cafeteria were completed. The anticipation of a new gym and swimming pool excited me. Above all, hope for the future glistened on those freshly

waxed floors. America's combat in Vietnam had just ended
the previous year, in 1972. Some kids my age had lost
their optimistic innocence. They grappled with the pain
of the war and the anguish of lost relatives. In contrast, I
flourished during the post Vietnam War years. My focus
and perseverance continued to develop.

Only students in grades seven through ten attended
the new school. Juniors and seniors, like my brother Tom,
went to Danbury. I quickly immersed myself in school
activities. Mascots, colors, policies, and more needed to be
chosen. The first sports teams were being assembled and I
was eager to play. I also wanted to be part of the student
government. Many leadership roles needed to be filled and
the class of 1976, the only class ahead of mine, didn't pick
up the banner. For me, it was going to be different. I had
the chance of a lifetime to be instrumental in creating a
legacy for future classes and generations.

Perseverance is admirable, but if you don't know what
you're striving for, you waste a tremendous amount of
energy. To channel that force, you must establish a set of
goals. I'm continually surprised by how few people, both
professionals and students, have actually established goals
for their day, week, year, or lifetime.

Years later, in business school, I had to write my own
eulogy—what I wanted to be read at my funeral as my
lasting memory. Though it seemed morbid, it actually was
an exercise in goal setting. When I tried to compose it, I
realized that even though I had established short-term and
medium-range goals, I had never formulated life goals.
As I worked on that assignment, I remembered an adage:
nobody on their deathbed ever says they wished they had
spent more time at work. I concluded that I wanted to be
known for a few simple things:

1. To have been a force for good, someone who made a difference in this world.

2. To have been a great husband and father.

3. To have been known throughout life as someone who generously gave back to society.

As a high school student, I wanted to be both a good student and a good athlete. I also wanted to make a difference in the new school. Its course was uncharted; it begged for involvement. Over the next four years, I was as involved as any other student. Good things started happening. Teachers, coaches, and administrators became active participants in my life. Finding the safety, warmth, and guidance at school that I didn't have at home, I blossomed. Encouraged to take the college prep curriculum, I discovered it to be both affirming and fulfilling.

Two years earlier, I had run for homeroom representative as a seventh grader. The sting of losing that election forced me to consider what had gone wrong. I probably was unable to articulate it, but during those years my world was all about me and how well I could do. I didn't give much thought to others' needs and desires. I realized I needed to care more about other people if I wanted them to reciprocate. Over the next two years, I became a better friend. I listened to my classmates talk about their own struggles with teachers and classes, about feeling powerless because they had no say in what happened at the school. In that spirit, I decided to run for president of our freshman class even though the thought of losing again worried me.

Each candidate had to form a four-officer ticket. Therefore, collaborating with talented, peer-respected individuals would improve my chances. I formed a team with three other classmates who were fairly popular, a combination of good athletes and outstanding students. I also believed the student body would most likely vote for the ticket that best represented their interests, not just the one that included the most popular kids. Sure enough, our team carried the vote by a wide margin. A landslide victory.

I served as class president and in the student government all four years, learning a great deal about leadership, delegation, and how to push things through the "system." That successful leadership experience whetted my appetite for even more responsibility. And I had learned that persevering and focused progress toward a stated goal improved the odds of a successful outcome. Sure it was demanding, but I embraced the challenge and pushed myself beyond my comfort zone.

Athletics also stretched me. I participated in three sports: baseball, basketball, and football. I served as captain on two of them, which also broadened my leadership training and goal setting. Opportunities for leadership on the athletic field are as valuable as any lesson learned in a classroom. Working with difficult personalities, balancing time management, overcoming setbacks, and making countless decisions developed skills that have fostered success throughout my life.

During high school, I also needed to earn extra cash both for my family's needs and for my own spending money. For example, regular medical and dental checkups had never been part of my parents' budget. Add to that the many trips to the candy store we kids had taken over the years without adult supervision, and all of us needed major dental work. I worked hard to pay for it.

My first job was at a local restaurant called Jim

Barbarie's. A few of my friends and I washed dishes for twenty dollars a night because we were under sixteen. Though not what I hoped to do for the rest of my life, it provided much-needed money and served as a sober reminder of what life could be like if I didn't work hard to get somewhere else. Once I turned sixteen, I got a "real" job at the bowling alley, distributing shoes to customers and doing some cleanup. Again, not the best job in the world, but it paid $3.25 an hour. Finally, I hit the big time. A wonderful man named Dave Donigian hired me to work at the town diner he owned.

I tried to save whatever I could for college just in case that was ever going to be a reality. Frequently, however, I used the money to pay for my younger siblings' dental work, to put a little food on the table, or to help my mother with the rent. The sum total of my savings by the time I graduated from high school was almost nothing. My three jobs had fulfilled their purpose, though: helping my family to survive and providing learning experiences that served me well in the future. I could've thrown up my hands and lived with what life had brought my way. Many people are faced with that choice every day and, unfortunately, many succumb to it. But I forced myself to persevere. In the midst of many frustrations during those challenging years, something inside kept me going, propelling me to rise above my circumstances.

Even though I succeeded in school, I still had no confidence about the future. A couple of things converged to make me think about becoming a dentist. A new dentist, Steve Hanrahan, and his wife, Lynne, arrived in town. Those two people, who later became my brother-in-law and sister-in-law, cared about me. Maybe I attracted their interest because I paid for my own dental work or because I was active in school, but I also think Steve saw a lot of himself in me. Though he is a very successful and well-established dentist today, he was just getting started then. He too worked several jobs as a teenager, saved his money, and clawed his way through college and dental school. During that time he also married, started a family, and served in the Air Force. Steve knew firsthand that life could be a struggle. He understood how much dedication it took to achieve a goal.

Since I had grown up with nothing, I dreamed of a better life. But I had no idea how to get there. Dentistry seemed to be a safe path that promised stability. Getting to college and graduating seemed to be the only obstacles. Nobody in my family, on either side, had ever graduated from college. My brother had started college, but by that time academics didn't motivate him anymore. He itched to make some real money, so he dropped out and started working. I was going to be different.

Fateful Encounter

With some good guidance, I decided that combining athletics and academics might make college attainable and affordable. But where would I go and for what purpose? Initially, I applied to the University of Connecticut, Princeton, Tulane, and a few other schools. However, I knew that without any financial help, I would end up at UConn. And that would have been fine—I would receive a good education and I was already acquainted with their baseball program and coach.

But then Tom's high school physics teacher, Jack Langford, approached me about another possibility, the

United States Naval Academy. I knew and trusted Jack not only because he had taught Tom and lived near our home, but also because he seemed to be a good and decent man. He first talked to me about the opportunity in September of 1976. I never imagined a school like that was within my reach—a prime example of not dreaming big enough. Having followed my development, Jack assured me the Naval Academy *was* within my reach. I had applied to Princeton simply because my godfather introduced me to one of their recruiters, but I also decided to give the Academy a shot.

I was immediately enthralled with everything the Navy had to offer: a great education, no tuition or other expenses, a chance to play major college baseball, the honor of serving my country, and a guaranteed job when I graduated. That all sounded pretty good except for one catch—a five-year military obligation after graduation. That length of commitment sounded ominous to a seventeen-year-old. But I completed all the required applications and took the mandatory physical exam to establish my candidacy. Next I faced a series of congressional selection committees, where I was competing against some of the top talent in the state. Toby Moffett, my congressman at that time, nominated me, and eventually I was appointed to the class of 1981.

I may never have accepted the appointment had it not been for my godfather, Dick Orefice, who paid for and accompanied me on a visit to the school, which was also my first plane trip. The Academy enthralled me. I had never seen such beautiful, old buildings. The Naval Academy fits seamlessly into Annapolis' historic landscape. In the hustle and bustle of that seaport city, I felt as if we were walking among the founding fathers during colonial times. Red brick, white granite, and manicured lawns surrounded us. Midshipmen scurried from one building to another with purpose and focused intent.

I also met the head baseball coach, Joe Duff, and watched a real college team practice. Familiar shouts and commands filled the crisp spring air. The Navy squad was being peppered with ground balls. I savored the sweet crack of the wooden bats connecting with cowhide baseballs. I could almost feel the satisfying thump of the ball when a fielder snagged it in his glove, then effortlessly turned and tossed it to a teammate. For anyone who loved the game as much as I did, the sights, sounds, and adrenaline rush of baseball are unforgettable.

It was a momentous, life-changing decision, but logic prevailed. Consequently, I entered the most unknown, unpredictable stage of my life—exuberant and also scared to death. For good reason, too.

On July 3, 1977, I drove to the Academy with a New Fairfield resident and returning senior, or first classman, Vinny Rossito. I had no money and no other way to get there. He was headed to orientation for what was called plebe detail. On the six-hour trip to Annapolis, Vinny tried to dump his entire previous three years of knowledge into my head. When we arrived, I stayed in a house affiliated with the Academy, where five other prospective midshipmen were also housed prior to Induction Day.

I had finally escaped the home life I despised, and I was about to embark on an exciting, challenging journey. However, I was also just three weeks out of high school, alone in a strange place with people I didn't know, and headed into an uncertain and clearly uncharted future. In short, I was petrified. The little solace I mustered came from watching the fireworks in historic Annapolis on the

Fourth of July and remembering why I was there—to serve my country and to pursue a better life than I had ever known.

Uncle Sam Takes Over

July 6 was Induction Day. Early that morning I strode through Gate 3, also known as Bilger's Gate. Its granite and brick walls anchor an ornate metal double gate with the Naval Academy seal and King Neptune's tridents adorning it. This was the infamous entrance where washed-out midshipmen, as legend had it, left the Naval Academy for good. My intent may have been bravado or naiveté, or maybe it was just the closest gate to my guesthouse on Maryland Avenue. I passed the Chapel, shaped like a giant cross, adorned with stained glass windows of famous naval scenes and heroes of the high seas. Its copper dome glistened in the sun. The walkways were laid with red brick. I passed numerous monuments that paid tribute to historic acts of personal bravery and momentous sea battles. I could hardly believe I would be included in the next chapter of naval history.

In any event, I arrived with over 1,300 other members of the class, the second one to include females. Academy officials immediately herded us into an assembly line for the distribution of uniforms and what seemed like everything else I would need for at least the next millennium. Each of us was handed two large white laundry bags which we stuffed with gear: shoes, sneakers, summer "White Works" uniforms, socks, underwear, books, belts and buckles, caps, gym shorts and shirts. I crammed so many items in the bag that it looked like

Santa's sack of toys on Christmas morning. That was just the first of many equipment "issues" I received during the next twelve months.

Commands I had never heard and steps I had never seen were drilled into me that warm, humid Maryland day. Relatively humane first classmen (seniors) marched my group across the grounds, called the "Yard," all day long. One endless step after another, initially in civilian clothes, then in issued old style "Pro-Keds" sneakers, and eventually in extremely uncomfortable black Navy-issue shoes. The blank gazes of all the bewildered faces belonged to my squad and platoon mates. Everyone was called Mr. or Ms.—a new experience for me. The other term everyone used, which I learned to hate, was "plebe." In the dictionary, *plebe* means "lowest class." Some brands of toilets even carry the moniker.

I soon learned that when someone shouted "plebe," something awful was going to happen. A phrase synonymous with trouble was "Plebe, halt!" One time I forgot to salute a senior midshipman as he passed by me. As I immediately stopped in my tracks and turned an awkward about-face, his nose came within a whisker of mine. With a wolf-like glare in his eyes and a string of colorful metaphors spewing from his mouth, he let me know how unprofessional I was, wondering why anyone would ever let me in "his" Navy. I learned quickly that one small mistake could lead to a much bigger problem. Being stopped by an upperclassman provided him with an opportunity to find other things wrong with my uniform: grains of dirt on my highly buffed shoes, a smudged belt buckle—any number of infractions, most of which weren't present before I encountered him. Within a few hours, I was sure of one thing: every fiber of my being was going to be tested to its limit.

We didn't officially belong to Uncle Sam until after the swearing-in ceremony at 6:00 p.m., or 1800 in military time, so our leaders were somewhat relaxed and friendly during the morning of that first day. I guess they didn't want any plebes walking out before the festivities even began. The list of what we had to do that first day was mind-boggling. After we received our first equipment issue in Halsey Field House, we went to other stations. At the barbershop we each received a buzz cut, which took about thirty seconds. At the bookstore we were given copies of bestsellers—at least for the US Navy—like the *Blue Jacket's Manual*, *Rules of the Road*, and the almighty *Reef Points*. We ate in the chow hall, King Hall, a cavernous room shaped like a big T, where 4,500 meals were simultaneously served. Within ten minutes the entire student body, or the Brigade as it is known, is seated. They quickly devour an endless array of proteins and carbohydrates. Because of the rigors of a midshipman's schedule and physical activity, each midshipman consumes over 4,000 calories a day. During that first day, I know I must have exceeded even that number!

Academy meals include lots of protein: scrambled eggs, toast, pancakes, and meat for breakfast; burgers, corn dogs, or pizza for lunch; roast, chicken, or some other meat for dinner. For dessert we consumed homemade tubs of ice cream, cakes, or other kinds of sweets. More food was laid on the table that day than I had ever seen, much less eaten.

In between stations our squad leader taught us how to stand, march, and salute. We donned our new "white works" uniforms and our sailor caps with blue rims. Everyone looked pretty silly in those outfits, but that was part of the message: "you may have been captain of this and president of that, but here and now you are nothing more than a lowly plebe."

He also forewarned us that for the next year we would sleep with *Reef Points*, the little booklet that contained thousands of tidbits of naval trivia, waiting to be absorbed by every plebe mind. Each day we had to memorize seemingly senseless, countless words. Included in the morning memorization ritual were two stories from the morning paper, menus for the next meal, famous naval quotes, ship designations, and Navy songs. Memorizing that trivia not only provided some genuinely critical information about the fraternal culture that had existed at the school since its inception in 1845, but it also increased my concentration and memory skills. Later, when I studied for tests, I realized my focus and ability to retain information had improved. That little book, which I still have, was attached at my hip for an entire year.

By six o'clock that evening, I was more than exhausted. I was nearly in a state of shock, reeling from all the new, quick-paced, completely draining activities. I had made it—barely. Then I, alongside my 1,300 new friends, raised my right hand and uttered these words:

> I, Bob Ravener, having been appointed a Midshipman in the United States Navy, do solemnly swear that I will support and defend the Constitution of the United States against all enemies foreign and domestic; that I will bear true faith and allegiance to the same; that I will obey the orders of the officers appointed over me; that I take this obligation freely, without any mental reservations or purpose of evasion; and that I will well and faithfully discharge the duties of the office

on which I am about to enter, so help me God.

Reflection Questions

1. Looking back, Bob can see that the invaluable attribute of perseverance was in his makeup even as a young boy. On a scale of 1 to 10, how would you rate your perseverance as a child? What score would you give yourself now?

2. When Bob was young, he was too embarrassed by his father and his home life to talk about his feelings with anyone. Did you face the same obstacle while you were growing up, or did you have someone you could confide in? Do you have someone you can confide in now?

3. Some of Bob's teachers, coaches, and administrators, as well as his godfather, took him under their wings and made a huge difference in his life. What adults made a positive contribution to your life when you were young?

4. High school was an "awakening" for Bob. What was the most positive experience you had in high school? What was the most negative one? How did those experiences mold you into the person you are today?

5. Bob recounts his first three jobs during his teen years. What were your first jobs? As you look back, what, other than a little money, was the greatest value of those opportunities?

Stay the Course

Most of the important things in the world have been accomplished by people who have kept on trying when there seemed to be no hope at all.
~ Dale Carnegie

I was both inspired and awed by the enormity of what had just transpired. The induction service had propelled me beyond thinking and talking about the military and its glory. I was going to live it. I had taken another step forward on my life's journey and felt ready for the challenge.

But no sooner had these thoughts passed through my mind than all hell broke loose. Proud family members swarmed around many of the newly sworn-in plebes after the ceremony. I stood alone in a sea of white uniforms, unable to share the momentous occasion with anyone. An unexpected emptiness swelled in my chest.

Fortunately for me, a typical Maryland sea squall rushed in from the Chesapeake Bay, pelting everyone with rain—perhaps a harbinger of the hardship that lay ahead. Everyone ran for cover, and for 1,300 of us that meant Bancroft Hall, our new home for the next four years. Bancroft Hall is the largest dormitory in the world—five miles of corridor, more than thirty acres of floor space, and 1,700 rooms spread across eight wings. I had only been in the building once that day. In the midst of 1,300 newly inducted plebes and hundreds of upperclassmen fleeing from the thunderstorm, I had no idea where I was supposed to go.

The moment I stepped into the building a horde of first classmen started screaming at me to get out of their territory, using every abusive name in their vast repertoire. My anxiety and loneliness turned to abject fear. My new classmates and I must have looked like a flock of terrified chickens, scattering helter-skelter about the coop after a hungry fox invaded it. I quickly learned what an upperclassman meant when he said, "Brace up"—push my chin as far into my neck as possible, creating multiple double chins. I was ordered to hold that position, standing at attention, while spit flew in my face as one "firstie" after another berated me with insults and threats. It didn't take a genius to figure out that the morning's activities had been a stroll on the beach compared to what that summer and the entire infamous plebe year was going to be like— something we all had heard about but for which none could have prepared.

Dripping with sweat from the humidity and soaked from the storm, somehow I made it to my room, still reeling from the thunderous onslaught of abuse. There I met my roommates. George "Hambone" Hammond, a local guy from Dundalk, Maryland, seemed like a fish in a sandbox. Smart yet unsure of his reason for being at the Academy, he was a soccer standout who never seemed to want the Navy or the Academy. His positive mindset coupled with his indifference to the upperclassmen's attacks taught me a lot about survival. Maybe it was his take-it-or-leave-it attitude that neutralized their torment. In any case, his friendship was welcome solace. Although his family's proximity and "chow packages" eventually endeared us to many an upperclassman looking to devour something more than a plebe's ego, George left the Academy after two years.

My other roommate, Mike "Hutch" Harber, became

my guardian angel. Hailing from Milton, Florida, he had already spent a year at the Naval Academy Preparatory School in Newport, Rhode Island. Consequently, Hutch had an invaluable year of tutelage behind him in the fine art of looking like a sailor. He had been recruited to play football for the Academy, and we formed an immediate bond that has continued to this day. I suspect it will last forever. He taught me everything about the Navy that I couldn't learn fast enough to satisfy my squad leader, Lon Yeary, a steely, chiseled wrestler who was headed for Marine Air after graduation.

And then there was me, fresh from small-town USA, dripping wet and wondering what on earth I had just done. My confidence and ability were tested throughout the first summer and all through plebe year, yet somehow I persevered. During one of our first group meetings, our company officer told us to look at the person to our left and our right. He then stated, rather bluntly, that one of the three wouldn't make it to graduation. His prophecy was accurate. By the time I graduated, the Seventeenth Company had shrunk from thirty-five to twenty-one, a 40 percent rate of attrition. The entire plebe class lost just about a third along the way—too heavy a price. The attrition rate, I'm glad to say, has decreased to less than 15 percent, the result of a great deal of effort, focus, and commitment to fully invest in the highly talented future naval officers accepted at the Academy.

Growth Curve

Stretched beyond my wildest dreams, I began to flourish. To maximize each midshipman's potential, the combined military, academic, and athletic equation pushed us every day. Only in retrospect can I see how much I benefited from it. Even the early hazing, complete with "white tornados" and "come arounds" contributed to my growth. In a "white tornado" several upperclassmen enter a plebe's room and toss everything out of the cabinets and closets so the plebe can perfect the art of folding clothes with military precision. The term "come around" was derived from the practice of upperclassmen requiring plebes to "come around" to their rooms so they could quiz them repeatedly about Navy facts and orders of discipline. Neither I nor any of my fellow plebes welcomed either term.

I had learned in high school to set goals for myself— making the honor roll, improving my batting average, delivering more tackles on the football field, and increasing my points, rebounds, and assists in basketball. At the Academy, I developed three lofty goals: to graduate with at least a 3.0 GPA, to earn a varsity letter, and to become a leader among my peers. I had been able to excel in a small high school, but at the Academy I competed with some of the sharpest students in the country at an elite school with a long tradition of fostering exceptional leaders and contributors to society.

I was fortunate to accomplish all three goals. I played on the first championship baseball team at the Academy in eighteen years, and during my senior season, we also won more games than any previous team. I was privileged to lead one of the six battalions in the Brigade of Midshipmen. With an average of twenty credits a semester, my academic regimen was rigorous. What I took away, beyond attaining a 3.0 GPA, will last a lifetime. Above all else, the Academy not only taught me about leadership but also gave me the opportunity to practice it at a very young age.

Into the Fleet

After graduating from the Academy, I served aboard the USS *Daniel Webster* (SSBN-626), a nuclear fleet ballistic missile submarine, or "boomer." Being a crewmember on one of the missile subs—nicknamed the "Forty-one for Freedom" because of their namesakes like Washington, Jefferson, and Lafayette—forced me to make numerous decisions that taught me invaluable lessons. At first, though, my responsibilities overwhelmed me. I was twenty-three years old with little practical experience, yet I led a division of missile technicians, some of the most experienced, capable, and critical of all sailors. They had more knowledge and experience about the Navy and their jobs than I could ever hope to master. Even more staggering was the stark reality that we would be responsible for pushing all the right buttons if the Cold War ever turned hot. On top of that, I had to learn to drive a $2 billion, 8,600-ton vessel with 150 lives on board—without hitting anything in the deep blue sea or in more shallow waters than I felt comfortable navigating.

My early days on board were tremendously invigorating and rewarding since I was finally able to put all my training into action. I had always been enthralled with the thought of following in my family's military footsteps and contributing to the security of our country. Serving on the USS *Daniel Webster*, I became, in my own small way, part of that safety net. Bearing that responsibility boosted both my confidence and my self-esteem.

One morning I went to the conning tower at the top of the submarine's sail as the junior officer of the deck, or JOOD. A sliver of the sun peeked over the hills surrounding the US Naval Station at Dunoon, Scotland, better known as Holy Loch, the body of water in which we floated. This area of the submarine, where all commands are given when on the surface, is a small, cramped opening at the top of the ship. Behind me were the periscope, antennae, and various masts.

With me on the tower were the skipper, a lookout, and the officer of the deck, or OOD—Dale Nees, who was as sharp as a tack and essentially became my mentor on board. He later distinguished himself as one of the youngest submarine skippers in the fleet, taking over command of the USS *Houston*, a fast-attack sub. What made Dale special was his strong desire to help other, more junior, officers to succeed. He spent countless hours with me throughout the different working spaces on the ship, investing in my growth and development. Lieutenant Tony Swerczek, our supply officer, had started as an enlisted sailor and worked his way into the officer program. He also willingly gave of himself to help others. The kind of leadership Dale and Tony exemplified set them apart from many other officers. Their commitment to teach me how to be a submariner accelerated my learning curve and enabled me to get more comfortable in my surroundings.

On that morning our ship was tied up next to the USS *Hunley*, a submarine tender designed to be a floating warehouse, stocked with virtually any part a submarine needed to be seaworthy. Leaving port was an intense and complex operation, requiring many members of the crew: the deck hands casting off the lines; the control room crew manning the periscopes, charts, steering, and radar; and the engine room crew ready at a moment's notice for power commands. For all its complexity, however, the

Navy tried to simplify the process with a checklist known as a standard operating procedure. Tugboats pulled the sub away from the pier, moving the 8,600-ton man of war sideways with little effort. Once in the channel, though, the tugs cast off and the ship navigated itself. Gaining some forward momentum is critical at that point since currents can do funny things to a ship over four hundred feet long, traveling with two-thirds of its surface below the water line.

The tugs cast off and I began to give the engine orders to stabilize the motion in the water. Suddenly, the sub started to shift in the channel. We couldn't have been more than a hundred feet from the tender, and a work barge was just ahead in the same position. Power was coming up, but there's always lag time between orders, power, and results. Making only about three knots, I saw the aft end swinging back toward the tender. The captain was horrified. His eyes darted around the deck, his mounting concern betrayed by the rising decibel level of his voice. But Dale remained calm. As the officer of the deck, he had control of the ship and all orders unless the captain relieved him. He calmly coached me through the process, keeping both his voice and the cadence of activity at normal levels. Not once did he speak or act as if we were in any kind of trouble.

We made some rudder corrections and ordered more speed. The submarine righted itself as if on command. In short order catastrophe was averted. The whole incident lasted about one minute. I breathed deeply, relieved that my career wasn't going to end before it began. No newspapers would be reporting that a junior officer caused enormous damage to a submarine by running into the dock.

That day I learned a lot about leadership during extreme circumstances and staying calm in a crisis. I was forced to leave my comfort zone, risk failure, and work through tough circumstances to accomplish a difficult task.

The next captain, Billy Heid, was a career sailor who rose through the ranks to eventually become a captain. He taught young guns like me a great deal about leadership. The USS *Daniel Webster* was his second command, and he gained my immediate respect because of both his enlisted roots and his leadership style. Rather than isolating himself in his stateroom, Captain Heid spent hours talking with the sailors where they worked or congregated: the Mess Hall, Torpedo Room, Missile Compartment, and Engine Room. He met us on our turf, a simple yet highly effective practice. In every interaction he was uplifting, positive, and supportive. And we responded.

Captain Heid wrote in my fitness report that I became his most trusted watch officer as I stood the daily mid-watch. During those lonely midnight to 6:00 a.m. hours, I was often responsible for taking the submarine to periscope depth. That depth is the most precarious position for a vessel—beneath the surface but shallow enough to either get sucked up to the surface or run into something on the surface. Those hours are also the most tenuous time for any ship: a decrease in activity means fewer eyes and ears are monitoring the vessel. Not to say we were in any danger—all the necessary watch stations were manned 24/7. However, fewer sailors were working on equipment or scurrying about the ship, so it might take longer to discover a problem. The daily mid-watch was about the only time the captain could sleep, so naturally he chose the person he trusted most to stand the watch and ensure the ship's safety.

Although Captain Heid never articulated why he trusted me, I assumed he recognized that I took my role seriously. I was also very knowledgeable about various procedures and actions to take, especially if a crisis erupted. Numerous drills prepared the crew to avert disaster if a fire, loss of power, or flood risked the submarine's seaworthiness. Everyone on board had a specific role to play in the drills. As a junior officer, I was required to give orders and work with the sailors to eliminate any threat. I also developed charts for the Captain's presentations to the Commodore and generally played the role of a conscientious junior officer. Therefore, Captain Heid relied on my judgment and actions in tight situations.

On board I learned how to lead a group of more experienced sailors, to remain calm in the face of danger, to take responsibility and ownership for my actions, and to appreciate the importance of detail orientation. On one occasion, I was the Duty Officer (in port officer in charge of activities on board). During those times, much equipment is maintained, replaced, tested, or updated. When someone wanted to work on a piece of equipment, the Navy used a Red Tag system to indicate when the power was turned off, which reduced the risk of injury. I had to coordinate the work schedule and ensure that no conflicts arose. A couple of sailors from my Torpedo Department wanted to work on one of the floating buoys that was housed beneath the superstructure of the ship with doors that opened to a ninety degree angle—the major portion of the doors ending up below the surface. Those sailors had asked me to tag out the buoy, but I said I couldn't because other equipment was already being tested.

About thirty minutes later, a request was made to test the buoy doors. I checked all the logs and there was no contradictory work going on, so I authorized the test. The next thing I knew, there was an emergency transmission topside. The two sailors, whom I had previously denied, had decided to work on the buoy anyway so they could get off the submarine that evening for a little R&R. When the doors being tested were opened, the two sailors were directly in their path. Since those heavy metal doors were hydraulically opened, nothing could stop them. Certainly not a human body.

I immediately climbed the ladder to pass through the topside hatch, not knowing what I would find and fearing the worst. Fortunately, young, fit sailors can move fast, especially when their lives are in danger. The two misguided young men were okay, except for a few lacerations. Disaster had been averted, but the two men had performed unauthorized work in direct contradiction to both an order and safe operating procedures. I disciplined the sailors but also breathed a sigh of relief. If those men had been trapped under the opening doors, they could have been severely injured, if not killed. Just one example of the potential hazards of operating a ship of war.

Many lessons and mistakes later, I finished my tour successfully, earned the Navy Achievement Medal, and reported to the Academy to serve as the athletic department's liaison to the academic department. I spent two very satisfying years there: coaching baseball, teaching midshipmen the art of boxing, recruiting for the Academy, and helping student athletes keep their grades "above water." Only a few years removed from their experience, I enjoyed the renewed camaraderie. Bonds forged over four years of challenges with classmates and teammates were strong and deep—not easily, if ever, replicated outside the confines of the Academy. Nevertheless, I also decided the Navy wasn't going to be a lifelong career for me. The appealing prospects offered by civilian life allured me.

A Woman's Touch

During my senior year at the Academy, I met a wonderful young woman on a blind date. Her bright smile, quick wit, and engaging personality attracted me immediately. Wearing my Navy letter sweater, I was first introduced to Lisa Lukon, the sister of my dentist's wife, in Tecumseh Court at the entrance to Bancroft Hall at the Academy. She was visiting Annapolis for the first time with her sister, Lynne, and her brother-in-law, Steve, close friends from my hometown. Not yet nineteen, Lisa was a sophomore at Fairfield University in Connecticut. She was a sweet, energetic dynamo with striking features characteristic of her Greek/Italian ancestry. Her long brown hair and big brown eyes reminded me of the famed Van Morrison song, "Brown Eyed Girl."

Our first date was fun but too short. I took Lisa to the Navy-Villanova football game. Navy was ahead 24-0 by halftime, so I relaxed and focused on Lisa for the rest of the game. After that, we went with Lynne, Steve, and his sister, Denise, to Georgetown in DC. That night Lisa's warm heart melted my calloused one. Her discerning eyes penetrated the emotional barriers I had built. But I liked it. And her. So I arranged to see her again, and our relationship flourished for the remainder of that school year.

Graduation came and went, and so did my common sense for a while. Fresh out of school and feeling like a big man on campus, I saw less of Lisa. In a town that loved to party, I was finally free to do whatever I wanted without the Naval Academy as my surrogate mother. Throwing our caps into the air affected us in a variety of ways. For example, right after graduation all of the new male ensigns and Marine second lieutenants grew moustaches—for two reasons. One, for the first time in four years we could grow facial hair. Two, and more importantly, it was really the only way to tell a recent graduate from a midshipman. Identifying ourselves as graduates, not students, was vital.

In my mind, submitting to any relationship constraints would restrict my fun. I wanted to enjoy all the benefits of being a single ensign. No strings attached. Parties, sailing, and nights on the town enticed me. But in the midst of the pleasure, satisfaction eluded me. Summer turned into fall as I awaited my orders for submarine duty. The glitter of the summer soon turned into the on-the-job reality of teaching classes, stepping away from the Brigade of Midshipmen, and waiting for the Navy training to start. I also missed Lisa. Trying to rekindle the relationship, I planned a trip to Connecticut, so I could see her when she started her junior year at Fairfield. When we finally connected at a party later that fall, our relationship quickly went into high gear. In November we got engaged, and in July of 1982 we were married. I was twenty-three. Lisa was barely twenty.

During the first three years of our marriage, Lisa stayed steady and strong while I was at sea. She was still attending college, growing accustomed to being a naval wife, and learning the importance of family, especially during times of separation. She made new friends with other Navy spouses in the military housing we dubbed "Navy Valley."

We couldn't contact each other while I was at sea, so we wrote several cards and letters to each other, sealed them, and dated them. Knowing we had a letter to open on a certain date gave us something to look forward to during the absence. Honestly, coming up with original words for fifteen to twenty letters at one time was difficult. But I did it. And using that system, strange as it was, helped us stay connected.

One other means of communication, which we considered a luxury, was a "sea-gram"—a few words on the teletype that spouses were allowed to send through the Navy submarine office. Sea-grams arrived two or three times during a tour of duty. They were "new" words Lisa sent directly to me, and I treasured them. Since they went through official Navy channels, the words were always G-rated. Still I hung on every letter and word as if I would never receive another message from her or hear her voice again. Those two-line messages were drops of cold water after weeks in the desert. Pure heaven.

A Dark Day

When Lisa and I moved to Annapolis for what turned out to be my last active-duty tour, everything seemed to be in place. Life was good.

We had waited until I finished sea duty to start a family. Once the moving boxes were emptied, we began trying in earnest. In the spring of 1985, Lisa glowed with joy and confidence as she carried our first child toward her June due date. Like every first-time father before me, I listened to her stomach, felt the kicks of the baby's feet, and relished the thought of holding our bundle of joy. Lisa did everything to ensure we would have a healthy baby: no alcohol or sweets; healthy, portioned meals; Lamaze classes with other naïve and expectant parents, which I could never skip. We furnished the nursery, decorating it with primary colors and stocking it with toys. Yes, everything was by the book. Filled with hopes and dreams, we looked forward to the responsibility of adding another life to this world.

Two weeks past her due date she went in for a routine non-stress test. Everything seemed fine except for riding the pregnancy out in the hot, humid Maryland summer. On the evening of July 6, the eighth anniversary of my Academy induction, Lisa went into labor. With her overnight bag in my hand, we rushed to the local hospital in our black Subaru. After she was admitted, we waited for the doctor to begin the preliminary tests. Anticipation soon turned to anxiety, however, as the doctor and attending nurse scurried for equipment.

The grim look on the doctor's face could have been me looking in a mirror. "I can't hear the heartbeat with my stethoscope," he said, "I'm going to try another method to determine the baby's health." He paused then added, "This happens sometimes so I don't want you to worry."

But we were very worried. And the doctor and nurses' concerned expressions and hurried actions indicated that our uneasiness was justified.

A sonogram confirmed our worst fears. Numb with shock, I could barely process the doctor's words as he uttered the unthinkable, "I'm sorry, but your baby is not alive."

Worse yet, Lisa still had to go through labor and deliver our child. After being in labor all night, what must have been ten to twelve hours, she delivered our little Brianna the next morning. With a cute little nose, all her fingers and toes—she was beautiful. But no newborn cries turned our apprehension to joy. Brianna's silence confirmed that everything was *not* going to be okay. Apparently, the umbilical cord had wrapped itself around her leg, cutting off her supply of oxygen. No one could have seen it coming.

The shock waves were immediate and overwhelming. Our world quickly became a living hell—an inferno of deep anguish and sleepless nights. Grief blurred the days, but a few events stand out. Jim Campbell, my commanding officer, visited us in the hospital. The fact that he was the only person who came had a dramatic impact on me. On the one hand, I never realized how awkwardly and ineptly people handle death, particularly a baby's death. On the other hand, I'll never forget the power of my skipper's gesture. He put aside his discomfort to comfort us. He didn't have to say anything. He was there and that meant everything. An unforgettable example of true leadership.

We had no choice but to pick up the pieces of our shattered lives. The burial at the Academy, attended by many dear friends, was incredibly painful. Lisa and I selected a military headstone, but we wanted it to stand out among the rows of white marble. On the back of the stone we had this epitaph engraved: "Forever she will live in our hearts." It was the least we could do to honor our little girl.

After the relatives had gone and the attention had dissipated, our empty house became a dungeon of despair. A baby was supposed to be nursing or crying upstairs in her little crib. But she wasn't. The following weeks were torturous. We both teetered on the edge of collapse. Support group meetings put us in touch with others in the same predicament, but it wasn't enough. Every time we walked down the street and saw a couple with a baby, the haunting emptiness returned. Baby displays in stores, laughter at playgrounds, and mothers pushing strollers all drove nails into our hearts. It seemed as though there was no escape. Where can you go to avoid the presence or suggestion of children? We knew the answer was *nowhere*, and in part that helped to repair our hearts. Drawing strength from one another, we kept the lines of communication open and focused on brighter days ahead, which was easier for me since I had my work to keep me occupied. For Lisa, being alone at home was especially tough. The Navy support staff was wonderful. They kept checking on us, gave us space, and made sure we were getting through the days.

In September, Lisa became pregnant again—a double-edged sword. We were ecstatic, of course, as the excitement of parenthood began anew. But what if something terrible happened again? A miscarriage at that point could have cratered us. As the months passed, we consoled each other and conversed with others about our ordeal. The wait was an endless emotional roller coaster ride. One moment we were doing the same expectant parent activities; the next, we were holding our breath, worrying what awful thing might happen and wondering if the baby's heart was still beating inside Lisa's womb.

On May 29, 1986, Cryssa Jean entered the world screaming at the top of her lungs—joyous music to our ears and deep relief to our hearts. In the years that followed, another daughter, Katie, and a son, Brett, arrived, generating all the love that any family could want.

We've all heard that time heals all wounds. Lisa and I made the long slog every day, as tough as it was, to get out of bed and face the world. We went to support groups, struggled through the malaise, and collapsed in bed every night. The next day we did it again. Little by little, the pain eased. We had other things to anticipate, and eventually we crossed over from pain and anguish to love and happiness again. We had two choices: give up or fight on. We chose to fight on.

Even though Lisa and I lost our first daughter and will never forget her, the years have brought us many happy moments—Cryssa and Katie getting married, Brett playing baseball in college. So as painful as it was for us, and as excruciating as it is for anyone to lose a loved one, we are proof that surviving very tough times is possible.

From Salutes to Suits

Back at the Academy, I was tracking the academic progress of student athletes, along with coaching baseball and teaching courses. During those years, Napoleon McCallum, an All-American running back, finished third in the Heisman Trophy balloting and later made it to the NFL. David Robinson, college basketball player of the year and eventual NBA superstar, also graduated from the Academy. The Navy, to its credit, placed a high priority, long before it was fashionable, on monitoring the athletes' academic progress. I spent a large portion of each day talking to midshipmen on their breaks and discussing issues with the academic dean and professors. Counseling those excellent young men and women, the future leaders of our military and the nation, was tremendously satisfying. Some of the best and brightest the country had to offer, they had an unquenchable thirst for knowledge and understanding. Helping them navigate the intricate maze of the Academy and watching their progress were worth every minute I invested.

As my tour wound down, however, I began searching for a second career. People in the military are isolated

from many elements of life in the outside world, such as
a looming recession and threatened loss of job security. In
1986, both President Ronald Reagan and the Cold War
were still going strong, and the Navy was on track for a
fleet of six hundred ships. Nobody was worried about
the state of the economy. As a result, I, like many others
in my military cocoon, had never bothered much with
anything in the civilian world. I had a lot of catching up
to do, especially since I didn't even know what profession I
wanted to pursue.

It was a stressful time for me, not unlike the
displacement I felt when I first arrived at the Academy. I
had no idea what adult life outside the military would be
like. The rules of the business world were different, and
I had no previous exposure to guide me. It would be like
entering a foreign country—not speaking the language or
understanding the culture.

Luckily I met Tom Wolfe, a fellow Navy grad who
was a partner at a recruiting company that specialized in
placing junior military officers. He worked diligently to
secure interviews for me with some of the best companies
in America.

In interviewing with the Pepsi-Cola Company, I met
Fred Koury, a staffing manager who had just recently
come on board with Pepsi himself. During the course
of the interview, Fred asked me if I had ever considered
human resources, since my most recent job at the Academy
consisted of recruiting, counseling, instructing, and
coaching. To be honest, the only thing I knew about
HR, or "personnel," came from a Dirty Harry movie, *The
Enforcer,* in which a precinct captain tells Clint Eastwood's
character, Harry, that he's transferring Harry to that
department in order to control him. In classic Eastwood

fashion, Harry responds, "Personnel . . . that's for idiots!" When the captain replies, "I was in personnel for ten years," Eastwood gives his patented scowl as he turns and walks away.[1]

But as Fred described the role of human resources and his own job within it, my interest was piqued. I liked the idea of being involved in every aspect of the business while working directly with people. Although I was excited about the Pepsi prospect, I continued my job search. I didn't know if Pepsi had a job opening that matched my naval discharge date. And even if a job was available, many other people had to give their consent.

One day while looking through the sports pages of *USA Today*, I read about a baseball talent evaluation process developed by a company in New Jersey called the National Collegiate Scouting Bureau. Most impressive was the way they mobilized pro scouts to conduct mini-camps across the country so they could evaluate high school baseball players—something that had never been done. Athletes paid a fee for the mini-camp. Then their evaluation was placed in a database that colleges could access for free in order to identify possible recruits. I called to see if they were hiring and was immediately invited to interview. It seemed like a great fit, a win-win. My job search ended when they offered me a position.

On the day I left the Navy and headed for New Jersey with Lisa and six-month-old Cryssa, our future seemed brighter than ever. I would be involved with something I loved—baseball. But this time I would be positioned on the business side of it.

On December 23, I reported for my first day of work.

---

1   *The Enforcer.* Produced by Robert Daley. Directed by James Fargo. Warner Brothers. 1976.

I expected to be greeted by a room full of coworkers, but I walked into an empty office. When the owner's wife eventually appeared—she had been meeting with the investment bankers—I could tell she was fighting back tears. She asked me if anyone had called to tell me what was going on. When I said no, she explained that the bankers had shut down the operation. My job no longer existed.

I was speechless for a few moments. As the shock subsided, disbelief emerged. Then apprehension. With no paycheck and no security, how would I support my family? I was devastated. Christmas came and went. To this day I can't remember one thing about the holidays of 1986.

In January, my deep-rooted survival instincts took over. I needed a job, so I started making phone calls. Fortunately, my prior contacts hadn't abandoned me, and amazingly I was working for Pepsi three weeks later. How? I'm not sure. I was at the right place at the right time meeting the right need. And I'll always believe that I was the beneficiary of divine intervention. At any rate, I began a career in business that has now spanned more than twenty-five years and afforded me experiences in other top companies like Home Depot, Starbucks, and Dollar General.

The experiences and lessons of those rewarding years will be woven into the pages that follow. Despite many setbacks, I have stayed the course—trusting in God, my family, my relationships, and myself. With much to be thankful for, I view the world and the future with great expectation. Many people cringe before defeat and never get back in the game because they fear they'll lose again or look bad. Can you relate? Hopefully, the rest of this book will help you see that you can achieve your goals in life by confronting and overcoming the obstacles you encounter.

Reflection Questions

1. What is the closest you have come to Bob's unsettling experience of Induction Day at the Naval Academy, followed by all the hazing he endured during his plebe year?

2. Did you move out of your family's home after high school? Where did you go? How did that experience help you? Do you have any regrets?

3. Bob began the discipline of setting goals in high school and, to a greater extent, at the Academy. When did you develop that habit? If you don't practice that discipline, what has prevented you from attempting it?

4. What are your current goals? What system do you use for setting, evaluating, and reviewing your goals?

5. Bob's first job out of the Academy was on a submarine. What was your first career job? What impact did your first boss, or bosses, have on you?

6. When have you suffered a profound loss? How did you deal with it? If you are still struggling, consider talking with someone you trust and commit to some positive action steps.

STEP *Up!*

Believe in Yourself

Nobody can make you feel inferior without your consent.
~Eleanor Roosevelt

On January 7, 2008, Howard Schultz, the iconic founder and mastermind of the modern-day marvel known as Starbucks, stepped up to a podium in the company's Seattle headquarters building. The large common area, its earthy color patterns similar to those in any local Starbucks store, was packed with employees. Eight years earlier, Schultz had turned the reins over to others, but the company's pristine image, along with its stock price, plummeted in 2007. I had speculated for some time that he or someone else would come in to run the company. On that Monday morning, in front of a crowd who adored him, Schultz announced that he was coming back to be the CEO.

A tall, thin, stately figure, with a big smile and confident stride, Schultz had a passion for people, high standards, and life. I often thought about his humble beginnings, which paralleled mine—his family had been poor, he grew up in the "projects" of Brooklyn, and he was willing his way to a better life. Anyone who has ever witnessed Howard Schultz in action knows full well that he is a man obsessed with the success of his company, and for good reason. He had built it from a small coffee bean sales company into a multibillion-dollar international conglomerate, which, by 2008, had ballooned to fifteen thousand stores in forty-four countries. Starbucks had known nothing but growth in sales and stock price since it had gone public in the early 1990s.

Schultz's decision to retake the helm initially stunned everyone, but soon euphoria spread through the ranks. This is not a small point. By then the company had exceeded 150,000 employees, called "partners." Wherever and whenever Schultz appeared in a store or in a corporate building, he was treated almost like a rock star.

During the days following his surprise announcement, there was a flurry of activity as talk throughout the building centered on his next moves. He had just replaced the CEO he had hired, and although the recent business results had taken a downturn in 2007, it had been only fourteen months since the company was touting it would grow to 40,000 stores—more than triple the number it had at that time—sending the stock close to an all-time high. Since I had joined the company in 2005, the stock had split and run back up to its pre-split price in rapid succession, and it had accelerated by more than 60 percent when the store growth announcement was made.

The company had just announced strong results for its fiscal 2007 business year when earnings per share had increased by more than 22 percent and same store sales, that true measure of business performance by operating unit, had grown 5 percent. But I knew the more recent results had softened. In the summer of 2007 at a US senior team meeting, Howard had interjected, "I'm concerned about our business on the current sales track. We'll be negative by September and I'm not going to let happen." But the slide continued, the stores finally did turn negative and just a few months later, there was a sea change underway. We all wondered what Howard was going to do.

I knew the shift in leadership might precipitate major changes for me. I had just completed my first year in the

Seattle office as the head of human resources for the United States, where the company still had most of its sales and profits—about ten thousand stores and more than one hundred thousand partners. My journey at Starbucks had started more than two years earlier when Dave Pace, Starbucks' global executive vice president of human resources, contacted me. Dave and I had briefly worked together more than twenty years previously when we were both at Pepsi. Saying that he thought I would be a great fit for the company and a leading candidate to succeed him when he eventually stepped down, Dave convinced me to make the leap from Home Depot to the Starbucks office in Atlanta in September of 2005.

Adding to the drama of Howard's announcement, Dave had just recently stepped down as the head of human resources (HR), and the selection process for his replacement was already underway. Both Dave and Jim Donald, the CEO at the time, had told me I was a leading candidate for the position. In fact, they said I was the only internal candidate being considered. As is often the case with high-level positions, Starbucks announced the opening to search firms who could objectively interview both internal and external candidates to ensure that the universe of top talent would be explored. Ironically, the week before Howard's announcement, the lead search team had scheduled an interview with me. All seemed to be moving according to plan: I believed I was the best candidate for the job, fully prepared to step into the chair and lead the Global Human Resources team to new heights.

After Howard's announcement, every employee speculated about what was going to happen next. My friend, Chet Kuchinad (the head of Total Rewards for the company over the previous five years) and I theorized the ways everything might unfold. Chet knew Howard well because he always presented the executive compensation proposals to the board, and Howard continued as chairman of the board after he gave up the CEO position. Howard is also passionate about healthcare benefits, so when he made numerous trips to Washington, DC, Chet often accompanied him due to his role in the company's benefits plans. Consequently, over that five-year period, Howard had become quite comfortable with Chet.

Chet and I discussed what Howard would do with the open HR position, arguably the most critical role for any new CEO to fill in light of all the people decisions and structural questions involved as well as the ultimate selection of an effective new leadership team. Suffice it to say that HR at Starbucks had been dysfunctional for a while, for reasons I won't delineate. That only added to the drama and speculation about Howard's next move. At one point, Chet told me he had recommended me for the job because he believed I was the most qualified choice, and he could think of no valid reason for going outside the organization.

As I walked by Chet's office on Thursday morning, January 10, we chatted again about what would happen next. Chet said he thought Howard was going to name either him or me as the head of HR that day. My thoughts began to swirl. Chet had been missing meetings in the weeks leading up to Howard's takeover announcement; however, I assumed he had been having confidential discussions with Howard since he was deciding on other top positions and needed lots of compensation support. I had never really thought Chet was a contender for the HR position, mostly because he never seemed interested in anything other than the compensation and benefits role. Something in Chet's calm, confident demeanor told me there was more to his comment than his words revealed.

Had Howard already told him what he had decided? If so, Chet didn't look like a man who had just been told he wasn't going to get the job.

Moment of Truth

I could have easily let that moment of truth overwhelm me. However, I had learned a long time ago to harness emotional reactions to things I couldn't control. Better to let the chips fall where they may. Later that morning, I was summoned from an all-day US leadership meeting to meet with Howard. As I waited outside his spacious office, my thoughts drifted to what I would say when confronted with his decision. My mind went blank. Standing on the doorstep of what I had worked so hard to achieve at Starbucks, I wasn't sure what I would say when Howard finally talked to me about it.

In actuality, I had joined the company with an aspiration to take on the top HR job, so I had been planning for weeks how to approach the responsibility if given the opportunity. A host of changes needed to be implemented—from structure to talent to process to cost management. The stock price had fallen precipitously over the last year as the economy soured, and none of the previous solutions seemed to be working. I had spent a career, almost twenty-one years, working toward this goal. In a few moments I would either start implementing my ideas or be forced to discard them.

The office door opened and Howard came out, dressed

in a shirt and tie—unusual in Starbucks' very casual environment. He had been doing a series of interviews with various media outlets and needed to look like the business icon he was. Howard is not just a visionary genius; he is also the Pied Piper of publicity. He can entice the media to write or talk about almost every move Starbucks makes. The name and logo have become synonymous with friendliness and just feeling good. Although the coffee is outstanding, it's the experience in the store that galvanizes customers. I too had been caught in the whirlwind of activity that swirled around this master of making the impossible a reality.

Howard held out his hand to shake mine and welcomed me into his office. I sat down on a white chair, he on a matching couch that surrounded a glass coffee table. We talked briefly about his announcement, the subsequent media attention, and his extremely busy schedule. He then said that a lot of people had been saying great things about me and that he greatly appreciated the work I had done in the company. He sat at the front edge of his couch to my right, leaning forward, his neatly knotted tie following the lead of his chin as he made his points. I had also learned that the best way to command attention and to be taken seriously was to sit forward with an upright posture, so I did.

"The simple truth is that I don't know you all that well," he said. "I want to get to know you better, but at this point I'm going with someone I know much better, so I'm putting Chet in the top job."

I couldn't say his pronouncement shocked me. As I tried to internalize his decision, he repeated that he wanted to build a relationship with me and wanted me in the company. Then he said, "I believe you can achieve anything you desire at Starbucks." He ended the meeting in a way that had made him so revered by others: "I need people that can help me turn this company around . . . people like you."

What do people say in such situations? Some, I suppose, voice their disappointment or point out the error of the decision. I said I supported Howard and would do my best to help Chet be successful. Howard said he needed that from me since he was very concerned about the challenging work ahead as well as the drama surrounding the human resources team. After assuring him that I would work side by side with Chet, I stood up, walked out of the office, and took the stairs directly down a few floors to Chet's office.

When I walked into his office, Chet was sitting at his computer. He stood and I smiled. He grinned with confirmation and extended his hand. As I shook his hand, I reached around his shoulder with my other hand, gave him a quick "man-hug," and congratulated him on being selected. Clearly, it was an awkward situation for both of us—no possible way to sugarcoat it. He said that he hadn't expected it and was going to need me. Then he asked what I was going to do. Though I certainly wasn't ready to make any long-term commitments, I said I wouldn't walk out on him. I would support him as best I could. He appreciated that. In the days that followed, I stood at his side and helped him outline the next chapter in the company's history, especially with HR. Chet decided to make several key changes that would require a great deal of leadership over the coming months.

In many respects, I understood Howard's decision. Like a new coach taking over a team, top leaders often install their own staff members. A huge task lay ahead of

Howard and choosing me would have meant one more variable. Who could fault him for selecting someone he already knew well and trusted?

Reaction Time

As the weeks passed, a number of people, some who had expected Howard to give me the position, asked me how I was handling things. In a company energized by large doses of emotion, many were amazed by my positive attitude. Some asked me point-blank how I was feeling. I routinely replied, "I can't control 100 percent of what happens to me, but I can control 100 percent of how I respond to what happens to me."

I simply refused to allow the situation to embitter me. And let's face it, I still had an important job to do with more than 100,000 employees in roughly 10,000 domestic stores —working through many issues to help the company return to growth and success. I owed the company, Chet, and Howard my very best. In many respects my response even surprised me. Three convictions kept me focused: I had confidence in my abilities, I knew at some point that I would probably leave Starbucks, and I was committed to excellence. Doing less than my best was not an option. To complain about my situation, to wallow in self-pity, or to hold grudges would have been both draining and counterproductive.

For the most part, confidence determines how we view the world. Trouble often starts with low self-esteem that translates into poor performance, lack of judgment, and falling well short of our potential. That is why believing in ourselves and what we can accomplish is so important, regardless of the obstacles. The successful people I have known or read about have taken the initiative to succeed despite obstructions. They have also relied on a network of contacts, spread out over their lifetimes, to help them reach their potential. Granted, your circumstances may be extremely tough, and you may be faced with more adversity than others. But if you don't take ownership for your future success, who will?

Small Steps

Taking steps to build self-esteem and to feel good about yourself is essential. On many occasions, I could have easily turned back or given up when I encountered a barricade. Instead I found an alternate route and persevered. How? It begins with understanding what I do well. Many people with low self-esteem criticize everything they do and blame themselves for anything that goes wrong in their lives. Small shortcomings balloon into major faults. A downward spiral builds momentum quickly. To break out of the cycle, begin with small wins. Find something—anything—to celebrate and start your ascent.

Everyone does something well. Even if it doesn't produce income, it can help you feel better about yourself. Ultimately, you'll be better at everything you do because your attitude will be more positive and your daily life more productive. Maybe you're a good listener. Volunteer to spend time with the residents at a nursing home. They would certainly appreciate the attention. Maybe you're an artisan—a seamstress, baker, or woodworker. No matter how unimpressive you may think the talent, your local church or charity can benefit from the sale of those items at a community bizarre. Maybe you've always wanted to get a college degree but could never find the time. Start with one class. One thing is sure, whether you do nothing and stay miserable or you do one thing and reach for happiness, time will march on. You'll grow older every day. So why not use that time to do something to improve your self-worth?

For example, about the time I was leaving the Navy, many of my Annapolis classmates were well on their way to earning graduate degrees. I too wrestled with that tough decision: go back to school or enter the real world. I knew I wanted an MBA at some point, but I decided to work for Pepsi instead. For years, job commitments and my young family consumed virtually all of my time. The probability of going back to school faded. When I was transferred to Pepsi's corporate office in New York, I realized the window of opportunity for me to get it done was closing quickly. Whether or not I went to school, by the end of my assignment in New York I would be four years older. So in spite of some protests from my wife, Lisa, I enrolled in New York University's night MBA program. I made a deal with Lisa and our two young children: I would try it for one semester. If it became too difficult, I would give it up.

That first semester was tough, very tough, especially taking three classes after being out of school for nine years. I seriously considered quitting. But I had achieved that one small victory—a completed semester. I took the next step—semester two. After three and a half years, twenty-three courses, countless lost weekends, and numerous commuting miles, I finished what may be the most grueling endeavor of my life. It all started with a dream, a glimmer of hope, one small win, and then downright perseverance. But I did it and the achievement will always be mine. Two other people on my staff at Pepsi also went back to school to fulfill dreams they had of achieving that elusive goal. So not only did I get satisfaction and self-esteem from my accomplishment, but I also felt the added pride of knowing that I inspired others to do the same.

Do whatever you can possibly do to give yourself a feeling of accomplishment and watch your outlook on life change. It might be a major goal, like earning a degree, or something much different, like volunteering time at your child's school. In every case, the hardest part is taking the first step. Once you do that, the rest will come much more easily.

Getting where you want to go and building your self-worth requires discipline too. Without it, I couldn't have completed my MBA, continued to grow in my career, and juggled all the components of my life. Is discipline hard to attain? Of course. But virtually anything can be learned. Discipline is a habit. Some habits are good; others are not. Good discipline is a conscious effort to improve your well-being. It demands both sacrifice and planning.

Earning my MBA meant missing a lot of sporting events and dinners at home with my family, plus I couldn't always muster that extra effort at work. I needed to be highly organized in planning my days: I attended school two nights a week year round, coached my daughter's T-ball team, and tried to stay on top of all my other family and work responsibilities.

How did I do that? Part of my method involved what I had learned aboard ship in the Navy. First, I made a list of all my tasks since trying to remember everything in my head increased the probability of missing something. Second, I prioritized the tasks in order of importance and the length of time I needed to complete them. Finally, I considered the interrelationship of one task to another and factored in which tasks could be done in sequence. I also took a simple, but helpful, time management course at Pepsi. I highly recommend courses like Franklin/Covey that help people better juggle their busy schedules. The final piece of the puzzle was discipline—monitoring my progress, checking off finished tasks, and ensuring that the next item on the list was completed.

Without discipline, I couldn't have done it. With discipline, you can't help but feel better about yourself. You begin to control your environment rather than allowing it to control you. And guess what? The downward spiral ends; an upward spiral begins. With each new win, you feel better about yourself.

Reflection Questions

1. Bob hoped, and even expected, to be promoted to a new position; instead, someone else got the job. When have you encountered a similar kind of disappointment? How did you react? Do you feel better prepared for the next challenge?

2. We can't control 100 percent of what happens to us, but we can control 100 percent of how we respond to what happens to us. How are you responding to life's unexpected curves?

3. How would you characterize your level of self-esteem? How hard is it for you to believe in yourself?

4. Bob maintains that discipline builds self-worth and that it is a habit that can be learned. Do you agree or

disagree? What is your attitude about discipline?

5. Bob notes that building our self-esteem and feeling good about ourselves starts with focusing on what we do well. What are your gifts and strengths? How could you build on them in a way that both contributes to the world and enhances your self-worth?

Marathon Strides

*There will be days you don't think you can run a
marathon. There will be a lifetime of knowing you have.*
~Unknown

The concept of a "bucket list" was made popular by
the 2007 movie of the same name. Jack Nicholson and
Morgan Freeman star in the film as two terminally ill men
who take an exotic trip to fulfill a list of things they want
to do before they "kick the bucket." Running a marathon
was one of the items on my bucket list. Maintaining a
positive attitude and adhering to a disciplined training
regimen were critical components in accomplishing that
goal.

In June of 1997 my nineteen-year-old niece, Wendy
Hanrahan, then a student at James Madison University
in Virginia, told me she was going to run in the Marine
Corps Marathon, a race held each October in Washington,
DC. Though the prospect of running with Wendy excited
me, I also realized I only had four months to train.
Although I had been an athlete all my life, I had never
done any distance running. I wouldn't even say that I had
good stamina. In fact, I couldn't recall running more than
four miles in one outing, so how could I possibly complete
a marathon?

The first and last battles to win in every war are the
ones in your head. I had to believe that my thirty-eight-
year-old body was capable of running a marathon and
that my mind was disciplined enough to make it a reality.
Three other factors also contributed to the challenge: I had

just begun a new job at Pepsi's corporate headquarters in Westchester County, New York, I was coaching my two daughters' softball team, and we were building a house. Life couldn't have been any crazier. I was moderately fit, but at my heaviest weight ever—218 pounds. I often thought about losing weight, but I could also list plenty of reasons regular exercise wasn't feasible. I had to admit, though, that recreational exercising hadn't been working for me.

On the other hand, I was a person who set goals and completed them. I had a job that required less traveling, and I could draw on the vitality and motivation of my niece who was half my age. (Wendy interned at Pepsi that summer, so we were able to train together until she returned to school.) I also had Anne Tuite, a fitness director at Pepsi and veteran of six marathons, to coach me. Talk about the planets aligning! My best opportunity to cross a marathon off my bucket list had arrived.

Preliminary Tests

The initial outings were as grim as I had anticipated. My day began at 5:00 a.m. so I could meet the "Pepsi team" at 6:00 a.m. They were younger, more physically fit, and serious about the sport of running for distance and time—a group of running thoroughbreds. Several were regular marathoners; all of them routinely ran shorter races. The first week of four-mile training runs exhausted me. Getting back in the habit of working out every day was grueling. My knees were sore, which probably had something to do with having cartilage surgery on both knees earlier in life. Muscles I didn't even know I had ached. I also became really tired later in the day. Focusing on work became difficult, and my eyelids became heavier with each passing minute as I sat in my office staring at the computer screen. In short, the first couple of weeks were agonizing, and I didn't feel one step closer to running 5 miles, much less 26.2 miles.

Persistence and the thought of watching Wendy complete the race while I watched from the sidelines kept me going the next couple of weeks. Then something amazing happened. The pain in my knees, which had constantly nagged me for the last five years, began to fade. I needed less sleep at night, and waking up in the morning became much easier. I didn't even need an alarm. My sense of accomplishment increased with each day and additional mile. I felt stronger and more alert than I had in a long time. Five-mile runs turned into seven-mile jaunts and then eight-mile excursions—up and down hills, in the dark, rain, fog, and traffic. I became a person with a mission.

The first real test was a fourteen-mile run in August. Even though I had been running regularly—farther and more often than ever—I was still far behind the others in my conditioning. For the first six miles I stayed close to my team, but I already felt winded and my leg muscles burned. I fell behind the pack after that and soon was running alone on the back roads of Westchester County, New York. Because Anne had placed water along the way, I remained hydrated. But at ten miles I needed rest, so I started walking. The last four miles took me as long as the first ten, but I finally made it back to the Pepsi office—two hours and forty-five minutes after I had left. The good news? I was still standing. The bad news? I had a lot of ground to make up if I was going to be ready for the big one.

I needed a more disciplined regimen. Wendy had left to return to college in September, so we had to finish our training in different cities. Even on business trips, I would have to squeeze in more than three or four miles. With the summer behind me, I worked in runs almost every day. The lofty goal of completing a marathon definitely motivated me. On tough days when weather challenges, a heavy workload, or back-to-back meetings created obstacles, I still ran. Discipline drove me. Even my diet improved as I honed my body into better shape. But the most amazing difference was the way my mind zoned in. Initially, I wore a headset and listened to something in order to fight boredom. As the weeks passed, I no longer needed distractions. Even though I was running two to three times farther, my mind stayed focused. Every run became just another segment of my daily routine. Running eight miles with ease, I tried to fathom how spending an hour or more on the road every day had become so effortless.

My next big test was a twenty-one-mile run in early October. The first obstacle was finding the course off the back roads of Westchester in the predawn darkness that Saturday morning. Our small Pepsi group was joining a group of runners from a local running club on a great course along one of the reservoirs that feed New York City, complete with an iron bridge and scenic paths along the water. Towering rock walls and vibrant fall foliage made it even more spectacular.

After the first leg of ten miles I still felt pretty good, though I was clearly among a different league of runners. I could tell that my fuel tank was running low. One runner, a veteran of five marathons, asked how many times I had done a twenty-mile run. When I admitted that it would be the only one I ran before the marathon, he laughed and said, "You're going to get killed!" If I had met those guys before I started training, they would have talked me right out of it. But at that point I was able to disregard them since our goals were so different. I was training to finish the race; many of them were training to break three hours.

The run did prove to be quite a challenge. I thought about slowing down to a walk several times after I passed thirteen miles, but water stations kept me going. The last few miles turned out to be another barrier, but I endured and managed to limp over the bridge, finishing in three hours and eight seconds—the slowest time in the group. After several minutes of cooling off, however, I felt fine the rest of the day. Another quiz passed on the road to taking the ultimate test, I assumed.

The final exam was only three weeks away, so my mind zeroed in on judgment day. After clearing the twenty-mile hurdle, I knew I could run a few more miles and cross the marathon's finish line. But something happened in the next two weeks that deflated my confidence. My legs didn't recover like I expected. A week after my long run, they still felt like rubber. Wanting to finish my training on a strong note, I struggled through an eleven-mile run. Those eleven miles hurt more than the twenty-one. I also felt a slight pull in my groin and at that point, I could have rationalized myself out of completing the event. But after more than three months of injury-free training, I refused to withdraw just before the race. I rested my legs for a few days and then did a few four or five mile runs, but I still felt less than ideal.

Adding to the mind game was the fact that Anne, my training partner and coach, had sustained a flexor muscle injury during a 350-mile bike ride for AIDS from

Boston to New York, which forced her to withdraw from the marathon. I was so close, though. Nothing was going to keep me from running that race. Anne met with me the week before the marathon and encouraged me to keep going, to recognize how close I was to completing something few ever attempt. Three days before the race, I ran my last four-mile training route. The day before the event, I traveled to Washington with my wife, Lisa. Wendy and her parents traveled separately.

I had participated in numerous athletic competitions —even championship games. Each time those proverbial butterflies had waltzed in my stomach. But not this time. In the past, I also had trouble sleeping before big games, but the night before the race I slept soundly. My mind was focused on one thing: completing the marathon. Waking up at 5:30 a.m., I ate a banana to avoid running on an empty stomach, and I drank lots of water to prevent dehydration. All week I had been preparing my body with steady doses of carbohydrates and liquids, which served me well on race day.

Race On!

Wendy and I met at her hotel, seeing each other for the first time since she had left for school back in September. We were both ready to run. Some of our friends and family members, who had come to support us, were eager to see us achieve our goal as well. It was a cold morning, in the forties, cold rain drizzling down on us—a potentially discouraging scene that was all but invisible to me. My mind had already activated a much-practiced race focus. We boarded the shuttle that transported us to the starting area. There we put our gear in a tent right next to the Iwo Jima Memorial, that iconic tribute to the Marine Corps, which immortalizes the moment the US flag was raised on Mount Sarabachi. As I headed for the starting line, along with more than eighteen thousand other runners, my mind sharpened to a razor's edge with a single-minded determination to complete the race.

A definite air of pomp and circumstance hovered over the event. The starter of the race—Secretary of State, Madeline Albright—was whisked into position in a police-escorted limousine. I wasn't wild about running in the rain and navigating a slippery race course. Sure enough, during "The Star-Spangled Banner" I felt the rhythmic rap of raindrops on my skin. But it didn't rattle me. I blocked it from my mind. At that point, I had one goal—the finish line.

What did concern me was "hitting the wall"—that point of the race when runners feel like they've slammed into a wall that prevents them from continuing. The specter of the wall haunts every runner, though I did my best to ignore it. However, any thoughts about the enormity of the event dissipated when a group of Penn State students walked into the starting area. All of them were wearing Nittany Lion blue T-shirts with lighthearted, motivational slogans plastered on the back:

The 1997 Marine Corps Marathon:
Mile 13: I hit the wall!
Mile 20: I thought I was going to die!
Mile 22: I thought I was dead!
Mile 26.2: I realized that I was too tough to kill!

A smile spread across my face and broke the tension. Any kind of encouragement would help me run a few more miles. I sparred with the "wall" one last time. I knew that most people began to walk or drop out at mile twenty. That wasn't going to happen to me.

The starting gun echoed across the rolling rows of headstones at Arlington Cemetery, although it was somewhat muffled by the heavy, moist air. Ceremonious cheers erupted from the crowd, but Wendy and I stood still. We were behind thousands of other runners and wouldn't be able to move for three or four minutes. Finally we began jogging, stride for stride, like everyone else.

Vice President Al Gore and his daughters were in the field, but we never even caught a glimpse of them. We had plenty of other people to watch, though. Most runners wore bright colored, logoed shirts. Some wore costumes—dressed like Superman, clowns, and even Groucho Marx. (He couldn't have been a competitor, though, because he walked through the crowd with the contorted walk made famous by the actor.)

Putting our name or a slogan on our jersey to help the crowds lining the course keep us motivated was one of the coaching tips we had been given. Many runners had zany names or slogans. All along the route spectators held hand-made signs, which named specific runners and displayed encouraging messages. I simply put "Navy" on the front of my shirt, which I discovered was a fairly common choice as were the names of the other branches of the military. Wendy put her name on the back of her jersey. We found out almost immediately that the fans watched the runners as they approached, not as they passed. Humorous to me, but much less so to Wendy, was hearing "Go Navy!" dozens of times during the race. Wendy had to settle for a few well-wishes from fellow runners. They read her name just before they passed us—something that happened more times than we could count!

When we reached a spot between the one-mile marker and the two-mile marker, we saw the leaders on a reverse path on the other side of the highway that served as our course. Seeing them run so fast and effortlessly, already closing in on mile three, was a little disheartening. Elite marathoners maintain a five-minute-mile pace throughout the entire race—a mind-boggling thought for an amateur runner like me. Realizing that I still had twenty-five more miles to go, the challenge ahead seemed overwhelming. However, Wendy and I kept each other in good spirits and maintained a steady ten-minute-mile pace.

The rain fell steadily, and the chill factor hovered in the low forties. My Navy tank top seemed like a good idea when I chose it that morning in the hotel, but my exposed skin became frigid as the raindrops pelted me. Remaining limber in spite of the cold was a constant struggle. I knew if I slowed to a walk, the elements would win and my muscles would stiffen.

On the one hand, running through the historic streets of Washington was a constant motivator as we passed one monument after another. Seeing the Kenyan leaders of the race, way out in front as we passed by the Pentagon, I marveled at their speed and stamina. On the other hand, battling the wind, rain, and cold along the Potomac River was a low point for me in the race. My sneakers were taking on water and getting heavier. What I wouldn't have done for a dry pair of socks!

Mile after mile went by. Wendy and I didn't speak. Each of us cycled through our own mental mantras. I repeated a series of reinforcing motivations from taking

one step at a time, to picking out a person in front
of me to keep pace with, to reminders of the sense of
accomplishment that awaited me at the finish line.

We also needed to conserve energy, and both of us had
our own internal demons to conquer. It would have been
easy to just stop. So many other people along the route
dropped out and moved to the side of the pack. Like the
Sirens who enticed Odysseus and his crew in Homer's *The
Odyssey*, the ease and comfort of the sidelines kept calling
out to me. But just as the wily Greek hero plugged his
crew's ears with wax to block the Sirens' song and ordered
them to tie him to the mast so he could hear the singing
but not be drawn to it, my mental focus tightened to
achieve the equivalent effect. And Wendy was my symbolic
mast. Another temptation avoided.

Wendy and I also picked key milestones to divide the
long race into many shorter runs. The first major milestone
was the one-mile marker. Then it became the five-mile
marker, the thirteen-mile marker (halfway), and so on.

Hitting the Wall

Around the halfway point, I felt a blister emerging on my
left foot. Momentarily, I wrestled with the possibility of
it nagging me for the remaining thirteen miles. Runners
go through lots of doubt and pain during this war of
attrition. I really had the same two choices one always has
in these situations—succumb to the pain and the misery
or fight through it. I was determined to resist the urge to
quit. In a grueling test of will, the mind can demonstrate
phenomenal discipline. I don't think I sensed the pain of
the blister for more than a minute before I regained my

focus, and just as quickly as the negative thoughts came, they vanished. I fought on. Seeing family members and friends at different points in the race also helped Wendy and me remain motivated.

The second half of the race took us beyond the cheering crowds, out of the intimacy of downtown DC, and through a park that paralleled the Potomac River. On a warm, sunny day it would have been picturesque; in the pelting, frigid rain it was a grueling battle against the elements. During that long trek, more runners started walking and others dropped out. Wendy and I ran behind a platoon of Marines whose cadence calls and songs provided us with a little levity and motivation. More importantly, the "Few and the Proud" served as a wind block that made those gusty riverbank miles a little more manageable.

We finally made it out of the park, but before we reached mile twenty we had to conquer the first sustained uphill climb. The combination of the elements, elevation gain, and leg weariness punished us more than we could have ever imagined. Raindrops mingled with the sweat pouring down our faces as we gutted out step after step. A mantra I employed many times throughout the race, but never more than during this stretch, was "Put your left foot in front of your right foot and eventually you'll be there."

As I passed mile twenty-five, a sense of completion surged through my aching limbs. Little did I realize that the next 1.2 miles would be the longest and hardest stretch I would ever run. The last mile seemed endless. Finally, I saw the finish line, shrouded in a sea of runners that, by their good fortune, were ahead of us or already done. Step after agonizing step, Wendy and I inched forward. As novice marathon runners, we were totally unprepared for the last two-tenths of a mile—another uphill climb. Who were they kidding? I could barely keep my body erect, much less run uphill! But up we climbed toward the sound of cheers and loudspeakers, a sure sign that triumph was within our reach.

The last leg was a whirlwind of excitement. Cameras clicked and people cheered as each runner crossed the finish line. Wendy and I locked arms and strode across it together, not knowing our exact time but guessing it was around four hours and twenty minutes. We were both exuberant but too weary to show it. The finish line was a sea of silver thermal blankets that had been passed out to all the runners—who definitely needed them that day. All of us had been given an automatic timer that we needed to return. And then Wendy and I approached the Marines who were giving every finisher the coveted medallion. Once those badges of honor had been hung around our necks, we gave each other a high five.

With a crowd of fourteen thousand finishers and twice that number in friends and family members, the area was wall-to-wall people. Finding our families was the next challenge. That took almost an hour, followed by another hour trying to exit the racecourse. Chilled and famished, we walked a mile or so to the Metro train that transported us out of the city and to our car. My legs had stiffened by that time, like quick-set cement. The additional post-race exertion had depleted any energy reserves I had. That certainly wasn't how I had expected to celebrate the completion of my first marathon!

After a few hot showers and about three days of rest I felt somewhat normal, though the incredible sense of accomplishment buoyed my spirits for weeks. The pride of completing that marathon has never faded. It mattered little that my time of 4 hours, 40 minutes, and 22 seconds placed me at number 9,821 out of 14,005 finishers (about 4,000 dropped out before the finish). I had set a goal, a very challenging goal, and completed it. Wendy and I had persevered to overcome obstacles and had attained something we could never lose—finishing a marathon. We had believed in ourselves, had been helped along the way, and had succeeded. We even crossed the finish line ahead of Al Gore!

Scratch one item on the bucket list. Just like I learned in my early Navy days, keeping a list of things to do, this time related to lifelong desires, is worthwhile. The marathon also reinforced the power of tenacity and focus. Wendy and I completed the event and 4,000 others did not. Probably the most important lesson was discovering how far we could extend ourselves beyond the normal routine of life if we put our minds to it and committed ourselves to its successful completion.

Our culture applauds and exalts highly accomplished people who make what they do look easy. But what we rarely consider is all the hard work that precedes the accomplishment. I have never met a significantly successful person who doesn't have a story that includes hard work, determination, perseverance in spite of difficulty, and tenacity in the midst of disappointment. These are the people we want to associate with, absorbing as much as we can by observing what they do to succeed.

Reflection Questions

1. What are a couple of items near the top of your "bucket list"?

2. Soon after Bob began to run regularly, he felt better
    than he had in a long time, confirmation that he hadn't
    been exercising enough. If your body could "speak,"
    what would it say about how you've been treating it?

3. Whether or not you have entered a literal marathon,
    what situation in your life has had "marathon"
    challenges?

4. What accomplishments so far in your life have been
    the most gratifying? Is there something that you
    learned or took away from that experience that could
    make a difference in your present obstacles or future
    goal setting?

5. Bob emphasizes the importance of a support system:
    the members of the Pepsi team, Wendy, and Anne
    while he prepared for the race as well as the fans,
    family members, and friends who cheered during
    the race. Who provides you with support and
    encouragement? On the flipside, whom do you
    support and encourage?

6. In "Believe in Yourself," Bob encouraged readers to
    take manageable steps toward building their self-
    esteem—volunteering at a nursing home or a school,
    making something for a church or community bizarre,
    or taking one class toward a potential degree. What
    step will you take that in turn will reward you with a
    wonderfully satisfying feeling of accomplishment?

The Power of Influence

It's easy to make a buck.
It's a lot tougher to make a difference.
~ Tom Brokaw

Being in the Navy forced me to learn that I needed to trust both the system and other people because I wasn't always in control. First, I needed to believe that all the challenges and mental anguish I endured the first summer in Annapolis were part of a grand plan to shape me into both a better person and a more effective leader. Having had no prior personal exposure to the military other than family stories, that was clearly a big leap, especially when every day was a battle of wits.

A second example was the life-and-death trust required during a week of flight training in Pensacola, Florida, while I was strapped into the "Dilbert Dunker," made famous in the movie *An Officer and a Gentleman*. The makeshift cockpit simulates a plane being ditched in the ocean as it submerses pilot candidates upside down in a pool of water. The experience is not just disorienting; it also puts all the pilot's body weight on the safety straps, making them difficult to release. If I had been on my own in the ocean, panicking could have been deadly, but in the Pensacola pool I quickly learned to trust the divers who were there to make sure I didn't drown.

A third test of trust occurred while I was on board the USS *Saratoga*, a battle-tested aircraft carrier. Given the chance to climb into the backseat of an F-4 Phantom fighter jet, I experienced the thrill of going from zero to more than 160 miles per hour in about two seconds. Three days before I arrived on board, one of the jets was launched off the deck, but the connection that holds the plane to the catapult, called the bridle, snapped and sent the plane over the front of the ship into the water. The pilots had about a half-second to decide whether or not to eject. Fortunately, when I watched the video of the incident, I noticed they wisely chose to eject and were quickly rescued from the sea. If they hadn't ejected, they probably would have been killed since the jet entered the water at an extremely high speed and immediately went under the one thousand foot vessel.

With that in the back of my mind, I climbed aboard and watched intently as our plane was moved into launch position. Following the obligatory salute to the launch crew, the jet hurtled down the deck until we were airborne and on our way to take our patrol station. I had to trust quite a few people that day, most of them less than twenty-five years old: the pilot in the seat in front of me and the many talented sailors who maintain the jets and the gear used to launch them. But it was certainly worth it.

Part of feeling good about yourself involves being around others who help you to do so. We all need affirmation to help us overcome life's obstacles. We also need role models to show us the way to a better, more productive life. Everyone can recount tragic stories of individuals who never reached their potential because no one affirmed their good qualities, or, as Stephen Covey always preached, no one sees them in light of who they could be rather than who they are today. Early in my life, I accidentally stumbled across some very good people. But I also realized, as I grew older, that learning as much as I could from others was a key to improving myself. A serious error that many people make is to ignore the power of associating with smart, energetic people—not to lean on them as a crutch but to hitch themselves to their successful practices.

Surrounded by Good People

When I was growing up, I was anything but confident. In fact, I was shy, introverted, and mistrustful. By the time I went to first grade, I knew my family was nothing like the families depicted on *The Donna Reed Show* and *Leave It to Beaver*. My older brother Tom and I attended Holy Redeemer Catholic School in Freeport, New York. You may not think the strict discipline of a parochial school and the resulting fear of authority would create an environment that built confidence. Yet the young nun who served as my first grade teacher was the first person I remember having a positive effect on my life.

Midway through that first full year of school, our family moved for the third time in less than twelve months because my alcoholic father couldn't hold down a job. My mother was caring for two nursing children under two and was pregnant with my youngest sister, so my dad had to drive Tom and me to school. And because he was working at yet another construction site somewhere, he had to leave home very early. So Tom and I rose before dawn and dressed ourselves in our uniforms—gray pants, white shirt, clip-on tie, black shoes, and navy blue sport coat. Then Dad dropped us off at the school well before it opened. Its locked gates prevented anyone from entering the grounds until a half hour before school started. As we stood there, homeless people sometimes approached us looking for a handout. Imagine our fear, a six-year-old and his eight-year-old brother, waiting for the gates to be unlocked.

Fortunately, one morning a few of the nuns, including both my teacher and Tom's, noticed two little boys sitting outside the school doing mostly nothing, certainly not completing unfinished homework. After they discovered why we were there so early, they asked us if we had eaten. We often left home without breakfast since Dad was usually rushing around, threatening to leave us behind if we didn't hurry. When we told them we hadn't eaten, they invited us—much to our surprise—into the convent. The formerly shrouded world of the nuns was opened to us, and to our shock and disbelief, those bastions of discipline and sanctity treated us with warmth and care. When they gave us bowls of Cheerios, we realized they genuinely cared about our well-being. After that, the way I related to my teacher changed drastically. If the nuns cared enough to reach out to a lonely, hungry boy, I could certainly do my schoolwork to show my gratitude.

My experience at the convent is my earliest recollection of recognizing the good in people. God knows I have run across my share of misguided and destructive individuals, some of them even being close friends or family members. Anyone can take the victim's perspective: we can conclude the world is full of bad people and the only way to protect ourselves is to isolate and insulate ourselves from the harm others are sure to cause us. But despite the abundance of evil in the world, there is more—much more—good than anyone could ever hope to tap. The difference is attitude: our attitude toward people and how much we invest in our relationships with them. Every interaction with a person is a learning opportunity. It may not be a good experience, but it can teach us something nonetheless. Much of the burden of learning belongs on us, however. We must seize opportunities when they present themselves because we may not get many of them.

Early in life, these learning opportunities often come from teachers and coaches. All of us will be exposed to countless people over the years, most of them trying to influence us in one way or another. Some individuals take the path of least resistance and follow the lead of others wherever it takes them, many times the wrong way. Others fight the temptation and surround themselves with friends and associates who provide a positive influence and help guide them to a better place. I have generally made a conscious effort to surround myself with smart, challenge-oriented people who have strong values. As a result, I have received some wonderful guidance just by being willing to listen to others and learn as much as possible from those interactions.

Throughout my school years, I was blessed with teachers who showed great interest in my development—no doubt in large part because they appreciated my positive outlook and thirst for knowledge. The best teachers weren't the ones who made it easy for me in class, but those who challenged me every day. Like most kids, I didn't always appreciate those teachers. But in retrospect, they taught me the most.

One influential teacher was Ray Wixted, who taught me in both junior and senior high school. He took a genuine interest in his students and helped them learn in a challenging and rewarding environment. He was both tough and well-liked. A rare combination. He wouldn't tolerate any mischief in his classroom, yet he was always willing to help a student in need. His compassion and commitment made every day special and left a deep impression on his students.

For example, he taught me how to play chess when I was in the sixth grade. The school had just started activity clubs once a week in the middle school, and he convinced me to give chess a try. I had never owned a chess set, and it seemed like Mr. Wixted was speaking a foreign language when he explained it. Consequently, I wasn't all that interested at first. But he knew I was competitive, so he compared it to athletics. A mental contest, he said, rather than a physical one. He gave me lessons during the activity hours, and slowly but surely I absorbed it. I enjoyed both its competitive elements and the strategy involved. Playing chess also improved my focus in class and helped me retain more information, which surprised me. Mr. Wixted didn't have to invest that time and teach me the game, but he took advantage of the opportunity to help me become a better student.

Probably the greatest influence on my life through high school was Walt Novak, my gym teacher and baseball coach for six years. A Vietnam veteran, he was tough like a drill sergeant, yet also tremendously committed to the kids he taught and coached. From the time I was in seventh grade until I finished high school, he taught me how to play baseball—and play it well. But more importantly, he became the missing father figure in my life during those critical teenage years. I spent a lot of time in Coach Novak's modest home. Because he knew how unstable my home life was, I often had dinner at his house with his young family after baseball practice.

In the early 1970s, teachers and coaches were paid so little that many, if not most, held second jobs. Coach Novak's other job was cleaning the floors in a local pub just over the New York border, one I knew intimately from my adventures with my father. How ironic that the man who was my mentor and father figure cleaned the floors on which my father and his buddies spilled their drinks. I even woke up at 4:00 a.m. so I could help Coach clean the bar, and then he drove me to school.

Another significant person in my life was Joe Duff, the stodgy disciplinarian of a baseball coach at the Naval Academy. Arriving on the banks of the Severn River in Annapolis in 1953, Joe devoted the next forty-one years of his life to the development of young, impressionable midshipmen and won 595 games as a coach, a monumental accomplishment. Short on praise and long on fundamentals, Coach Duff was very demanding. He had high standards for himself and his players, and he pushed us to attain them. He coached me for four years, but I never felt I measured up to his standards. He was not a warm and fuzzy guy around his players. Plus, he knew that in a confined and structured environment like the Academy he needed to maintain strict discipline on the field and when the team was on the road.

Coach Duff did have a dry, humorous side, however. Every lesson on the field and in life became an analogy to the softening of American ideals. Like many athletes, I thought Coach Duff had eyes in the back of his head since he never seemed to miss a mistake on the field. As a first baseman, I often made throws to home plate, and if it was ever off the mark, he let me know it. He had many funny quips, but one he often yelled out for all to hear was "Bobby, how hard can this be? You know, home plate hasn't moved since Abner Doubleday invented the game back in the 1800s! C'mon now, make that throw!"

Baseball, Coach Duff said, was the ultimate sport in the sense that individuals couldn't hide. Nobody but you could field a ball hit directly at you, and when you were at the plate it was you against the pitcher—*mano y mano*. He held to the fundamental philosophy that people learn the most through failure, which then ultimately makes them successful.

Heroes Among Us

All of us find heroes in unsuspecting places, even within our own families. My father-in-law, George Lukon, acquired only a tenth-grade education. Like so many of his generation, he was shipped overseas during World War II. After fighting the Nazis in Italy, George returned home to begin a new life. He didn't have special abilities that the rest of us don't possess. But he did have a vision of what he wanted to achieve. Moving from the ice cream business to burgers (before McDonald's was a household name), and finally to the travel industry, George made the same mistakes that many people make. However, he learned from those mistakes, took risks, and eventually became quite successful. Throughout his life, George has been a loving husband and father, and over the last thirty plus years, a wonderful father-in-law and grandfather. He has always given helpful advice, spent quality time with the grandkids, and more than anything else, led the effort to keep the extended family connected so that we could build long-term relationships with one another.

When I was a child, my maternal grandfather, Frank Smith, emerged as my greatest hero. He still is. His family came from Germany in the 1800s and settled, like so many other immigrants, in New York. He dropped out of high school in 1913 and became a coppersmith. In 1916 he enlisted in the New York National Guard searching for adventure, and he was almost immediately called up to the US Army. Grandpa was attached to the unit, commanded by General John "Black Jack" Pershing, that was sent to fend off the wily bandit, Pancho Villa, at the Rio Grande borders of Texas and Mexico. From there he went to France to fight in "the war to end all wars," now known as World War I. Upon his return, Grandpa jockeyed between the New York City police department in Brooklyn, the Army Reserves, and two more wars, World War II and Korea.

When he shared his war stories and run-ins with the gangsters of the day, Grandpa always included a moral. To a young boy with no fatherly role model, the lessons carried great impact. He talked about a strong work ethic leading to a stable income and a positive attitude resulting in a better state of mind. He told us to go to bed early and get up early—not until much later did I learn that Ben Franklin espoused that philosophy long before it came from the mouth of my revered grandfather. Though Grandpa wasn't more than six feet tall, his experiences made him seem larger than life to Tom and me. As I studied pictures of him in military uniform, I saw in him everything I wanted to become. And I did everything I could to make him proud.

During my first summer at the Academy, Grandpa sent me three letters, some of the precious few I received. He wrote all of them while his body was stricken with colon cancer, which took him from me a few months after my induction. Each letter had a profound effect on me—the primary reasons I survived that grueling summer.

The first letter arrived barely a week after I had been inducted. I didn't know it at the time, but Grandpa was already sick and surely in great pain. In spite of that, he still had the tenacity, humor, and thoughtfulness to write to me during what he assumed would be the darkest days of both his and my life. Here is that letter:

> 7-12-1977
> Dear Bob:
> Just got your address from your Ma. She said you lost 5 lbs already. Oh well! That's to be expected. I know they will pour it on for a while, and that it's awful hot down there. I was stationed in Washington for a while, and it was hot. Hope you will be settled down soon and get used to it. I am sure you will, and will come out with flying colors. As they say, the first 100 years are the hardest. Keep up the good work, son, and keep smiling. Good luck, and Anchors Aweigh! Grand Pa

I had always known in my heart that I had a connection with my grandfather; however, until I received his letter, I didn't realize that he had such a big place in his heart for me. No words can convey the power of that moment. After spending almost a week under constant scrutiny and a steady diet of people in my face, his letter was the fuel I needed to pick me up and keep going.

I called Grandpa not long after receiving the letter to tell him how I was doing. It was like he was my guardian angel, letting me know that everything would work out fine. He recounted his boot camp days in 1916 and how tough it had been to fight along the Mexican border because of the heat, dust, rattlesnakes, and bad guys. He encouraged me to keep my head up and persevere. He never mentioned that his health was deteriorating quickly.

Any hope he had of winning the battle against cancer was gone, but the two other letters he sent that summer were life preservers of hope for me. I wrote to let him know how I felt about him as well, and then we were able to talk on the phone again. It seemed very difficult for him to accept the affirmation and affection I expressed to him in my letters, but when we spoke on the phone, I knew my written expressions of love had hit home. Grandpa wrote the last of his three letters on August 16. The last words he wrote to me expressed his never-ending positivity: ". . . So son, keep up the hard work, with the flag flying high and all guns blazing. Thank you so much for the letter and keep smiling and your head high."

One sweltering September day, a battleship gray Navy car pulled up to the baseball field during practice. A chaplain and a first-class midshipman got out and walked over to Coach Duff. After a brief exchange, Coach called me over and said I needed to go with them. When I asked why, they simply replied that the head chaplain wanted to see me. Though the field is only about a mile and a half from the chaplain's office, the ride seemed to take an hour. I had heard just a few days earlier that Grandpa was sick, but I had no idea how sick. Once I was ushered into the chaplain's office, he told me that he had just received a call from my uncle with the news that my grandfather had died the previous evening. The chaplain added that my grandfather was a courageous soldier, that he had lived a very fruitful life, and, fortunately, that he didn't suffer long.

The words hit me like a torpedo. The pillar of strength in my life had vanished. No more letters or phone calls— nothing but memories. My eyes welled up with tears, and I wept.

Without any money, I didn't know how I would get to the funeral. Then I was told that one of the club teams was taking a trip to New York for a competition, and I could hitch a ride with them. For one of the few times since I had been inducted, I was allowed to leave the Academy grounds, and although the circumstances were painful, getting out was a blessing. Even in death, Grandpa was looking out for me.

The funeral, with full military honors, proved to be incredibly moving. I had never been to a funeral, much less one with all the pomp and circumstance of a military ceremony: the flag-draped coffin lying at the front of the church as the priest conducted the funeral mass; the honor guard, in dress uniforms with white gloves, folding the flag with such precision at the grave site; the firing of a three-volley salute at the cemetery with shell casings spinning rhythmically out of the chamber with a distinct clang after each shot; the bugler playing "Taps," the solemn military anthem of death. It seemed surreal, yet its grandeur was glorious. And since I was in uniform, I could finally salute the man who had meant so much to me.

In my interaction with others, I try to remember the impact my grandfather had on me— his demeanor, lessons, and service to others as well as the time he invested in me. In some small way, I hope that I have even a fraction of that kind of impact on others.

Role Models All Around Us

Another person who influenced me positively was Tom McLoughlin, one of my coaches in Little League. Only seven years older than I was, Coach McLoughlin had a gift for teaching little kids the art of baseball. But what made him really special was the way he cared about us. He took time out of his full-time profession as a police officer to hit baseballs for hours to energetic protégés for no other reason than to help us improve. Owen McDonnell, my high school principal, also consistently provided guidance and motivation for me. He directly influenced me to pursue a Naval Academy education and eventually become a recruiter for the school.

John VornDick may be the most invested private citizen to support the military. Since the early 1970s, he has opened his home and spent just about all the income he has ever earned to support midshipmen at the Naval Academy. Over the years, he has probably enabled hundreds of midshipmen to survive the rigors of four years at the Academy by providing kindness, meals, and friendship. He was certainly a major reason I survived it. His home became a weekend respite for my friends and me—as plebes we were forbidden to talk outside our rooms, watch TV, or listen to the radio or records. Simple pleasures like hot dogs, vats of chili, TV, radio, and records at John's home allowed us to rest and relax like normal college students for a few hours each weekend. His legacy is one of complete selflessness and devotion to the welfare of others, a noble and high standard.

Colonel David Vetter, a career Marine from the Naval Academy class of 1967 who fought in Vietnam, had a profound influence on me during my Navy days—first as my economics professor, then as the varsity baseball officer representative, and finally as the dean of admissions. He demonstrated the impact we can have by building up others. I never heard him speak an unkind word to or about another person. He has always been the kind of man who finds something positive to say about the ones under his tutelage. For me, he was always good for a slap on the back after a good play on the baseball field and a pick-me-up after a mistake. I distinctly remember him telling me how proud he was when I was selected as a battalion commander. To be a competitive athlete who was also chosen by the "military brass" to lead others at that level was an honor at the Academy. During the days when the Marine officers at the Academy had a well-deserved reputation for being hard-nosed and unyielding, Colonel Vetter was by far the most popular officer, probably because the midshipmen appreciated his positive attitude and constant encouragement. He could say those things because he took an active interest in us, which we both recognized and valued.

In spite of all the bad press he has received, Bob Nardelli, former CEO of Chrysler and the former chairman, president, and CEO of Home Depot while I was there, had a tremendous influence upon my life. Bob has a commanding presence—poised, confident, and smart. He doesn't have to say much to convey that he is in control of his environment, but he also displays a genuineness that sets him apart. Among the more endearing things about him is his love and support for the men and women of the armed forces. With Home Depot growing rapidly, the military was a potential source to bring quality talent into the organization. I was tapped by the head of HR, Dennis Donovan, to lead that effort. By the time I left the company, Home Depot was on pace to hire almost twenty thousand military vets a year and was touted by *G.I. Jobs Magazine* as the most military-friendly company in America.

I don't pretend to know what went on in the boardroom that led to the end of Bob's tenure as CEO of Home Depot and the severance package that created such big news. What I do know, however, is that Bob Nardelli was a driven yet accessible CEO who took a personal interest in me, my family, my career, and our shared interest in the military.

Rick Dreiling, the CEO of Dollar General Corporation since January of 2008, has been a great mentor since I began working for him as the head of HR. In his first year on the job, Dollar General set a sales record by exceeding $10 billion for the year, profits increased by more than $100 million, and same store sales, something that literally defines the health of a retail chain, grew by more than 9 percent. This is even more impressive in light of the fact that the United States was facing its toughest economic climate in more than twenty-five years, and perhaps since the Great Depression. Rick is the best I've seen at balancing both the numbers and the people. He not only understands the levers that drive business but is an exceptional people leader as well.

It has been exciting to be part of a company that experienced strife in the recent past but coalesced around a group of very different people who all share a common goal. Rick has been masterful in herding these strong personalities into a cohesive and highly effective senior business team. Although he deserves much of the credit for the company's recent success, he also knows and recognizes the contributions of those around him. Rick exemplifies what all great leaders possess: the awareness that they need to surround themselves with talented people whose collective strengths are much greater than the sum of the parts. Always bringing out the best in others, he knows how to motivate people while also holding them accountable for their actions. He has that rare quality, that gift, of making those he encounters—from the highest executive to the most junior store employee—feel special.

The last person I will mention is my brother Tom. Because of his adolescent rebellion, I worried about Tom throughout his teen years. After high school he enrolled in college, but he soon lost interest. Always enamored with law enforcement, Tom became a deputy sheriff in Florida and Louisiana for a time before returning to Connecticut. Fortunately, he had met someone in high school who would ultimately both change his life and become his wife. Pam Fiske was the catalyst of the lengthy process that turned Tom's anger and resentment into productive and positive energy that transformed him into a positive force in both his family and mine.

Although Tom was working close to home in Connecticut while I was at the Academy, he visited me often. His exposure to its environment had a profound impact on him. My friends became fond of Tom, always a loyal person, and he seemed to enjoy the camaraderie of the Academy. We became closer than ever, ironically, while we were living miles away from each other. Eventually Tom moved into electronics, became a partner in a computer refitting company, and is living the American Dream with a wife, two beautiful kids, and a house in the suburbs. He's even a recruiter now for the Naval Academy. Despite all of the obstacles, all of the abuse, Tom's resolute will and resilient determination enabled him to succeed. I have learned as much from him as anyone.

I could write an entire book on the countless friends, relatives, teachers, coaches, and coworkers who have had a dramatic impact on my life. But the point is that I opened myself up to learning from these good people. Did they have faults? You bet! Could someone choose to see those faults as repulsive warts and turn the other way? Most assuredly!

Too often we choose celebrities as role models, but we only see them on their stage. We don't see how they live off stage. Let me encourage you to find the admirable qualities in the people with whom you live and work. There is no better way to improve yourself than by learning from the good people around you. Don't be fooled into thinking that they don't exist. They do. Just open your eyes. And your heart.

Reflection Questions

1. Bob shares some rather dramatic examples—being strapped into the "Dilbert Dunker" and riding in the backseat of a jet launched from an aircraft carrier—of being forced to learn to trust in other people. What are some experiences that have helped you to learn that you aren't always in control and that you need to trust other people?

2. Do you tend to see the good, or the bad, in people? Would you like that to change?

3. Throughout Bob's life he has tried to make a conscious effort to surround himself with people who provide a positive influence. Do you agree that we have the opportunity, and therefore the responsibility, to make that choice? How do you feel about your track record in that regard?

4. Bob still treasures the three letters he received from his grandfather during his first summer at the Naval Academy. Can you recall a similar gesture that made a profound impact on you?

5. As you think about the various people you have
    encountered in your life, determine the three
    individuals who have had the most positive impact on
    you. What was special about them? List several ways
    you could emulate those qualities.

6. Bob makes several observations about important
    qualities for leaders. Which of those qualities speaks to
    you the most regarding your leadership roles?

Chase the Dream

You see things, and you say, "Why?" But I dream things that never were, and I say, "Why not?"
~ George Bernard Shaw

In 1983, Coach Jim Valvano led the North Carolina State basketball team, which had lost ten games during the regular season and finished fourth in the Atlantic Coast Conference, to an improbable national championship. During the championship game, the heavily outgunned Wolfpack beat the seemingly invincible University of Houston Cougars, nicknamed "Phi Slama Jama" because of players like future NBA superstars Clyde Drexler and Hakeem Olajuwon. Valvano's secret to success has a great deal of merit. In the locker room he hung a sign that read:

You + Motivation = Success

Valvano, who believed that motivation plays a key role in an individual's performance, defined motivation as "hard work, enthusiasm, and dreams." That NC State team pulled off one of the great upsets in sports history because an exuberant coach with a dream willed a group of individuals into champions by a simple philosophy.

When I was young, I dreamed of playing baseball for the New York Yankees. During countless hours of stoop ball, stickball, and baseball I plowed my way through the lineup. I also knew the players' statistics because I assumed that if I didn't know Mickey Mantle's batting average, how many home runs Joe Pepitone had hit, and Mel

Stottlemyre's ERA (earned run average), I couldn't be called a true fan of the game. So my friends and I spent hours memorizing the stats of our idols and dreaming of the day we would step into their shoes. But that was all it was—a dream. Never did any of us believe that it could actually come true. Those Yankees were supermen who could leap tall buildings in a single bound, who could hit and throw with their eyes closed. Even as I continued to play ball and improve my skills, I never really believed I could make it to their level.

That was a big mistake. The importance of education and job security was drilled into my head, but I never considered that the advice was coming in all directions from children of the Great Depression who had a limited view of the world outside their own backyards. I'm sure the lack of security in my own life played a big part as well. When you spend hungry, cold nights in different rented digs, dreams die. Having food on the table becomes the primary priority, sometimes the dream itself. No, making it to the big leagues was never more than a distant star in my universe, one that eventually collapsed into a black hole.

Hindsight Is 20/20

Not until after I entered the Academy did I realize that I had stopped dreaming too soon. My talent had progressed enough to get tryouts with some major league clubs when I was in high school, but those teams were seeking a broader skill set than I possessed. I wasn't yet fast enough or physically developed enough. Neither did I fully grasp at the time that I hadn't had the same exposure as many of my competitors. At Annapolis, our team not only played against well-known programs like Louisiana State, University of New Orleans, Southern Mississippi, St. John's, Old Dominion, and Creighton, but we were also competing against players who eventually made their mark in the big leagues.

Navy played in the Ivy League—at that time called the Eastern Intercollegiate Baseball League (EIBL) because of the inclusion of Army and Navy. One of the stars was Yale's Ron Darling, who played many seasons in the major leagues, pitching for the world champion New York Mets and later the Oakland Athletics. He and I happened to play collegiate ball the same four years. I also faced two great pitchers from St. John's University in New York: Frank Viola (who hit me in the back in a game at Navy), a future Cy Young Award winner; and John Franco, whose record of 424 saves ranks fourth on the all-time list of major league closers. Perhaps the best position player I played against was University of New Orleans' Randy Bush, who became a power hitter for the Minnesota Twins. Many other fellow competitors were drafted into the pros as well, but those were the most notable.

Surprisingly enough, Navy also had some great talent. With solid defense and a monster swing with a big thirty-three-ounce bat, Rich Seiler, our second baseman, became an All-American. Opposing coaches sometimes pulled their players off the field so they couldn't watch Rich take batting practice. Our rangy shortstop, Mike Mulliken—nicknamed "Pigpen" for his trademark dives into the dirt to get to balls—was an All-East player who should have been an All-American based on his selection to the US national team in 1980. Rounding out our infield was third baseman Jimmy Roberts, who eventually became a .400 hitter and an All-East selection as well. Our catcher, Jimmy

McKee, was a free-spirited live wire. He seemed very much out of place at the Academy, but he possessed the best arm I ever saw in collegiate competition. The outfield featured some outstanding players too: Steve Komlo and Steve Acklin eventually became All-East selections and Andy Loferski, the centerfielder during my senior year, an All-American. Phil Austen, my best friend at the Academy, who had a great sense of humor, was a standout from Port Jefferson, NY, who possessed a rocket arm and converted from shortstop to the outfield. I rounded out the position players at first base as a left-handed fielder who had learned to be a switch-hitter in high school—a valuable skill since I could hit well against both left-handed and right-handed pitchers.

Our excellent pitching staff lacked depth, however, and that proved to be our undoing in the 1979 NCAA tournament. We had talent—the team averaged .320 at the plate and won 75 percent of our games. In the four years I played, the varsity record was 87–29, not bad for a military school.

Three signature games for me during the regular season in 1979 stand out en route to Navy's baseball championship that year—the first one in eighteen years, which also sent Navy to the thirty-two team NCAA tournament for the first time in twenty-five years. One was our 22-0 blowout of Army at West Point's Doubleday Field (at the time, the most runs scored by either team in the history of the rivalry, dating back to 1901). Another was our 13-9 victory over the University of Maryland, a regional rival in the Atlantic Coast Conference, and my first and only grand slam at any level of play. The third was a 1-0, eleven inning, nail-biting triumph over the University of Delaware, the number twelve team in the country at the time. Against Army, our high-octane offense amassed five home runs, including a grand slam by our shortstop, Mike Mulliken, and a shot by All-American Rich Seiler that rocketed over the fence and hit the building across the street, a distance close to five hundred feet away. Our pitching ace, Paul Kelleher, threw a one-hitter to complete the day's domination. Our gutsy 1-0 win against Delaware pitted Kelleher against one of the best teams in the country, and although our bats were held in check that day, our defense and pitching was outstanding. Kelleher went the distance over all eleven innings, pitching a complete game and allowing only three hits in his masterful outing.

Facing My Fears

During those years, one of the biggest obstacles I encountered was facing Colin McLaughlin, a six-foot-six BB-thrower from the University of Connecticut, in the 1979 NCAA tournament. As the champion of the EIBL, Navy hosted the four-team Northeast regional, which also included St. John's (with Franco and Viola, two future major league star pitchers) and Nebraska, which had won forty-nine games that year. Held during graduation week at the Academy, the atmosphere was electric yet distracting, especially for the Navy seniors. We faced UConn in game one on a rainy day in Annapolis. Though the weather threatened to hold up the tournament, after some good grounds work the game began. The flame-throwing McLaughlin was on the mound against our ace, Paul Kelleher, who had beaten Delaware just a week before. Our team's early tournament jitters enabled UConn to jump out to a quick 3–0 lead, which stretched to 5–1 after three innings. At that point, black storm clouds surrounded the field and the prospect of completing the game looked bleak.

I had faced McLaughlin for the first time two years earlier in a high school all-star game in Waterbury, Connecticut. Playing in the NCAA tournament was stressful enough, but facing McLaughlin again actually unnerved me. He had not only made me look bad in high school, but he also had scared the living daylights out of me! He was big and hurled the white sphere close to one hundred miles per hour—all a batter was likely to see was a blur. And he frequently threw wild pitches. Though both of us were sophomores, McLaughlin was well ahead of me physically by at least six inches in height and probably thirty pounds. He was UConn's ace, an All-American, and I was the .250 hitter who batted ninth.

Since my opponent was right-handed, I stepped into the left side batter's box for the first time that day in a very critical situation. Already battling the enormity of the moment, I valiantly tried to forget the first time I had met McLaughlin in competition, but initially I was unable to shake it. I stepped out of the batter's box and took a few more practice swings. Once I stepped back into the box, my focus zeroed in on the pitcher, just sixty feet, six inches away from me on the mound. Every other possible distraction was wiped from my mind. I had one goal—get on base. We had runners on first and second with two outs. Scoring a run would keep the game close. I dug my cleats into the soggy clay with my left foot on the back line of the batter's box, searching for as much distance as possible between me and the blazing heat that would sizzle toward the plate. Even if the pitch was clocked at ninety-five miles per hour, I would have only a fraction of a second to react. And I was far from being the quickest bat in the East. All I could do was stand in the box and swing.

Drizzle pelted my helmet and dripped from its brim as I watched McLaughlin's massive, sinewy frame adjust to the mound, his eyes riveted on the catcher as he awaited the sign. He shook off one sign with his head, then nodded. He straightened up into his stretch position to hold the runners on base. Expecting his heater, I tried to stay loose, moving my bat back and forth across the plate like a pendulum, never taking my eyes off of his steely gaze.

Once the pitcher begins his motion, hitters shift their eyes to the point of release in order to identify what kind of pitch is coming. If the ball leaves the pitcher's hand and immediately moves above the release point, it's a curve ball. If the ball is released directly out in front of the pitcher's hand, it's a fastball, slider, or change-up. The next thing to watch is the spin of the laces on the ball, which helps the batter determine the exact pitch and hopefully gives him an idea of its speed. Each pitch spins differently in order to give the ball the movement the pitcher intended. With only a fraction of a second to react, a hitter needs to process all that information simultaneously. Successful pitchers find ways to throw the same pitch, but they spot it in different places around the plate and at different speeds, always keeping the batter guessing. What makes a good change-up so successful is that it leaves the pitcher's hand looking and spinning like a fastball, but it comes to the plate at a slower speed. Good hitting requires impeccable timing, and varying pitch speeds are designed to throw that timing out of whack.

McLaughlin, though, was a pure power thrower—not yet a master of the art of pitching. He was *all* power, or so I thought. Therefore, when his first pitch came in as a fast curve, maybe a slider, I was stunned! Few collegiate pitchers throw the curve ball much, and fewer still have the confidence to start a hitter's at-bat with it. Lucky for me, the ball moved a lot but was low and inside—the psychological game had begun. Even though the pitch was a ball, it made me think.

What McLaughlin didn't know is that our wily coach, Joe Duff, had taught all of us to "have an idea" at the plate. Coach Duff devoured percentages. He knew the fastball was the money pitch for all but a very few on the hill. He taught us to watch for the pitcher to make a mistake. Unless we had two strikes, we waited for that pitch. All bets were off with two strikes, but until then, good hitters stuck to their "idea." Invariably, the "mistake" pitch would be a fastball, and it might well come on the first delivery, so the hitter needed to be ready.

So by Duff's doctrine, my idea at the plate was to think fastball all the way. It didn't matter that McLaughlin's first pitch was a curve. I wouldn't have swung at it even if it had been a strike. But I didn't want to get behind in the count—every hitter's nightmare. All kinds of statistics prove that when a pitcher gets ahead in the count, he dominates hitters; when he gets behind, hitters make him pay. I was a career .300 hitter at Navy, and probably 75 percent of my hits came when the pitcher was behind in the count.

Baseball is a mental game. With runners on first and second, that first ball had given me a slight advantage at the plate. McLaughlin didn't want to walk me and load the bases, so I knew he was thinking "just throw strikes." Again he took the sign from his catcher, this time with no wave-off, and I knew it was going to be his best pitch, a heater.

Knowing what's coming is one thing; hitting it is quite another. Recoiling like a rifle shot, the white "dot" whistled toward the plate. I had to swing. Without hesitation, I committed all my muscles to meet the incoming missile. My torso turned as the bat swung through its plane, and my rear foot pivoted in place so I could strike the onrushing ball with the full force of my momentum. My head stayed down and my body coiled after the swing as all the forces were disengaged.

What should have been the thunderous whack of my bat hitting McLaughlin's pitch somewhere into the stratosphere turned out to be the hollow pop of a major league caliber fastball landing in the catcher's mitt. I stepped away from the plate, undaunted but frustrated. I had lost my advantage and perhaps had just missed the only pitch I could hit. Knocking the mud from my spikes with the bat, I tried to regroup and prepare for the next pitch. I still thought fastball, and after seeing me miss his last one, I assumed McLaughlin would just try to blow the rest of his pitches by me and send me back to the dugout just like he had done two years earlier. Once again I watched him look for the sign, and he quickly locked into his stretch, ready to fire the ball past me, like a cannonball. Again I swung my bat slowly across the plate, trying to use the confines of the batter's box to release the nervous energy inside me.

All I could think of was Coach Duff's baseball mantra: there's nowhere to hide. No assistance, no escape. Every player at the plate is an island. Everyone who has ever played baseball, at any level, has experienced the stark terror of being alone at the plate battling your worst nightmare. Big game, runners in scoring position, every at-bat crucial. But it's also the place that the best players want to be when the game is on the line—the place where dreams come true. That's how I viewed my battle against McLaughlin. I wanted to be the guy who made something happen.

Standing in the rain and mud I waited impatiently for the next pitch, which was not a fastball but a hard slider—similar to the fastball in speed and release but with much more spin and a break at the end of the pitch. Starting outside the strike zone, as so many of these pitches do, the change in spin forced just enough hesitation on my part to take away any advantage I had. The ball curved and dropped over the outside corner of the plate, just above my knees. Strike two. With the count at one and two, I had tumbled into a deep hole. McLaughlin was clearly in command. I faced the additional humiliation of stranding a runner in scoring position. Everything at the plate changes with two strikes. I choked up a couple of inches on the bat for better control, ready to swing at any pitch near the strike zone.

I dug my cleats into the dirt, realizing that any pitch in McLaughlin's repertoire could come blazing my way. I just wanted to put the ball in play somewhere, anywhere, to avoid the embarrassment of leaving men on base and slinking back to the dugout, head bowed in defeat. The sign came, the nod followed, the stretch ensued. McLaughlin uncoiled his body and rifled the ball toward home plate. I detected the slider immediately. He was trying to flirt with the outside part of the plate. I had to swing. Could I anticipate the break of the ball, time my swing perfectly, and hit the sweet part of the bat? My bat connected with the pitch on the barrel, and I immediately felt the rush of adrenaline and the sheer power of hitting the ball well—a line drive over the shortstop for a base hit in the opposite field. When such a moment occurs, the play seems to unfold in slow motion. I wanted to savor every millisecond. I had gone with the pitch as I had been coached so many times, and at that instant I realized that all the hours of practice, frustration, and dedication had paid off.

My part completed, I watched our runner on second, who wasn't real fast, get a late jump. But he needed to score to get us back in the game. Unfortunately, the throw from left field was accurate, the tag at home surgically applied, and UConn out of the inning.

I got another single at my next at-bat to drive in a run, yet we were still behind 5–4 at that point. Unfortunately, though, sheets of rain began to fall, and the umpire ended the game after six innings—an official game that wouldn't be resumed. Navy had rallied but fell short and lost a heartbreaker. With our momentum interrupted, we lost the next day to Nebraska and were ousted from the tournament. UConn won the regional tournament and advanced to the College World Series, an experience I would have loved, but one that UConn earned, especially since they defeated both of St. John's aces, Franco and Viola, to advance.

McLaughlin went on to be the number one pick in the January 1980 major league draft, and I had beaten him twice at the plate just six months before that. Several years later, when I was coaching baseball with Coach Duff at Navy, he said that he believed my battle against McLaughlin was the day I "arrived" as a ball player. I made a statement in a critical at-bat in the most important game Navy had played in more than twenty years. A high compliment from the man who was short on praise and long on discipline.

Don't Put All Your Eggs in One Basket

I accomplished something monumental that rainy day at the Academy. I overcame adversity even though I would have much preferred to win the game. I stared down a nemesis that had dominated me only two years before and made me look foolish. I triumphed by facing him and getting two hits (more hits than anyone else on our star-studded team). I never dreamed I would be in that position. On that day I realized that I could compete with the best players in America and that I had missed my opportunity to compete with them in the future because I hadn't perfected my craft. Playing baseball was "fun." I never thought that it could take me to greater heights.

My baseball skills helped me get into a great college. But I'll never be able to answer the "what ifs" about a professional baseball career. Striking the balance between wishful thinking and probable achievement is difficult because the odds are certainly long. According to Mike Trueblood of Galesburg.com Blogs, only .015 percent of high school baseball players (1.5 out of 10,000, or 1 out of 6,667) make it to the major leagues. Very long odds. Still, 750 athletes play professional baseball at the major league level (25 per team). They beat the odds. They play the game at the highest level.

Even if you pursue a dream, however, you can't put all your eggs in one basket. I'm so glad I concentrated on being a good student and going to college. Nobody can play baseball forever, no matter how talented they are. Everyone needs other skills to continue to succeed in the world. I'm not talking about school time, but rather all the downtime—the time many people waste, not doing much of anything or spreading themselves too thin over too many priorities.

And what if you achieve your dream? How do you stay motivated? The answer is simple: never run out of dreams. When you're searching for motivation to keep going, find another challenge. When Coach Valvano led his North Carolina State team to win the "big dance" in 1983, he became only the twenty-eighth coach to win a national championship. He then found out that only six coaches had ever done it twice. A new challenge.

Reflection Questions

1. When Bob was young, he dreamed of playing baseball for the New York Yankees. When you were a kid, what did you dream about doing when you grew up?

2. Bob thinks it was a big mistake not to believe that his dream could be fulfilled. Did you take any steps to fulfill your childhood dreams? Do you have any regrets in that regard?

3. In the batter's box, Bob faced not only a flame-throwing pitcher but also his fear of failure. When have you been thrown into a situation in which you were forced to stare down or relive past failures or challenges?

4. What dreams do you have at this point in your life? How can you pursue your dreams but also avoid "putting all your eggs in one basket"?

5. If you have achieved your earlier dreams, how can you become motivated to find a new challenge?

Take a Risk

My daughter Cryssa once wrote to Wendy Lawrence, a classmate of mine at Annapolis who later became a NASA astronaut in the space shuttle program. In her letter, Cryssa asked Wendy how she became an astronaut. Wendy responded that when she was young, about Cryssa's age, her father, Admiral Bill Lawrence (the superintendent at Navy while Wendy and I were there and also one of the finest leaders this country ever produced) had been a finalist for the initial space program. Unfortunately, he was disqualified due to medical reasons. (He continued to fly A-4 Skyhawk attack jets and was shot down over Vietnam, enduring over six years in a North Vietnamese prison.) But as a test pilot, Admiral Lawrence was a fellow Navy alumnus and a close friend of many of the first astronauts. Therefore, Wendy received firsthand knowledge about the space program from quite a few men who followed their dreams into space.

Think of Wendy's world: she knew Alan Shepard, the first American in space; John Glenn, the first American to orbit the earth; and Neil Armstrong, the first person to walk on the moon. From that point forward, she knew she wanted to become an astronaut. In her remaining adolescent years, Wendy excelled in academics, especially math and science, pursuing her goal to be accepted into the Naval Academy. She wanted to attend the alma mater of most of the astronauts, graduate near the top of her class, and then excel in the Navy to improve her chances of being accepted into the space program.

Wendy became an exemplary student and leader at the Academy. I worked with her directly since she was the deputy brigade commander (number two leader) and I was one of the six battalion commanders. I have always admired Wendy's focus, commitment to succeed, and ability to set a goal and achieve it. Without a doubt, Wendy possessed the resolute commitment necessary for an astronaut.

Shoot for the Moon

I had also thought about being an astronaut when I was young. But astronauts, like major league baseball players, were larger-than-life figures to an under-privileged boy growing up in a small town with little access to the outside world. I dismissed the notion that I would ever have that opportunity even after I entered the Naval Academy.

That was another mistake on my part. I'll never know if I could have accomplished that rare feat. But after seeing Wendy and two other classmates—Brent Jett, our brigade commander and valedictorian, and Kay Hire—make the space program, I often wonder about the commitment I could have given to such an endeavor. What is the difference between those three exceptional classmates and me? They weren't afraid to follow their dreams, and they had the discipline and commitment to achieve them. I, on the other hand, was content to take one safe step at a time, never venturing much beyond my perceived abilities, and ultimately too far away to reach for the moon.

However, on January 12, 1997, I witnessed the launch of the Space Shuttle *Atlantis*, piloted by my Academy classmate, Brent Jett. Being invited to the launch was a once-in-a-lifetime opportunity that I shared with my children. After trekking down to Orlando the day before the scheduled launch, we were nervous about a potential delay. The morning paper cautioned that the temperature might be too cold and that NASA was taking no risks after the 1986 *Challenger* disaster. Many other launches had been delayed for various reasons, including the weather; however, something told me that with Brent at the helm everything would go off smoothly. Even at the ripe old age of twenty-one, he had carried himself with singular confidence and poise as the Academy's brigade commander (senior student leader). Why would the launch be different than anything else he had done?

My body hummed with adrenaline and anticipation, much like I used to feel before a big game. Wanting nothing less than the best seat in the house for the predawn launch, my children and I planned to arrive just after the gates opened around midnight. We packed a cooler with every intention of conducting a tailgate party, just as if we were going to a Navy home football game. Once inside the complex, we parked the car and situated ourselves for the four-hour wait. As soon as I opened the door, I looked up and saw the bright spotlights shining on the spacecraft— majestic yet eerily still. Loudspeakers provided the play-by-play dialogue between the astronauts and mission control. Every time I heard Brent's voice, chills went down my spine. The voices sounded every bit like what I normally heard on TV, yet this time I actually knew who was speaking!

Anticipation mounted as the countdown descended toward T-minus five minutes and counting. My kids had fallen asleep, and I couldn't rouse them. When the countdown fell below two minutes, and I still couldn't wake them up, I did the only rational thing left to do—I pulled the kids out of the car and put them on the roof! Luckily, the early morning chill and the growing excitement awakened them. As the announcer reached the one-minute mark, I checked the angle of my video camera.

The next five minutes were probably the most dramatic moments of my life. Everything was a "go." The rocket ignition, liftoff, and elevation seemed to merge into one single, awe-inspiring event. The sound and shudder of the massive ship shook the ground and lit up the sky like the midday sun. Smoke billowed far and wide from the pulsating engines. The launch vehicle lifted reluctantly, like a groggy dragon, the millions of pounds of thrust pushing it ever so slowly into the starlit sky. Then quickly and smoothly, the shuttle accelerated to thousands of miles per hour, becoming a glittering disc in the dark sky before I took a single breath. Even as the craft rocketed toward space, following the contour of the earth and looking like a meteor, I could still hear Brent's voice over the loudspeaker. Tears streamed down my face as I absorbed the magnitude of the moment: nobody in the crowd would ever forget that sight, and the pilot flying that magnificent symbol of America's grit and greatness was my friend.

Neither my baseball nor astronaut dream ever came true, but other dreams did. Throughout my life, I have worked hard toward many lofty goals. For example, attending one of the service academies was a dream fulfilled, and my life has never been the same. I remember my grandfather espousing the virtues of an academy education and military career. I never disagreed with him, but I always thought it was just another unattainable star in my less than ideal universe. No one in my dysfunctional family had ever attended college except my older brother Tom; therefore, my immediate goals were to survive to adulthood and possibly earn an undergraduate degree. Something as lofty as attending a service academy seemed unlikely even though I never completely dismissed it.

I did, however, want to excel, so I continued to invest all my energy into academics and athletics, to what end I wasn't sure. Throughout my school years I continued to be enamored with the military, mainly because of my grandfather and, I must admit, John Wayne. Never quite certain what I was striving for, I kept coming home with A's on my report card and making all-star teams in athletics. Excellence seemed to be the ticket out of my unfavorable circumstances; therefore, I steered myself in that direction.

Pursuing lofty dreams is different from pining after pipe dreams—wishing something would happen but never really doing anything to make it a reality. Setting realistic goals and working hard to achieve them has propelled me toward greater achievements all my life: first with the Navy, then with Pepsi, and currently with a company and opportunities that seemed as fanciful as Peter Pan's Neverland when I was a boy.

New Horizons

In the winter of 1996–1997, I had just celebrated my tenth anniversary with Pepsi. My career had been progressing well, and I had just completed the first year of my second tour back at corporate headquarters in New York. Coming back to the East, after spending three years in Colorado, had been a priority for Lisa and me. Our three kids were growing up and we wanted to establish some roots closer to family. Brad Thomas, a longtime mentor of mine, had approached me about coming to headquarters as the director of safety and risk for Pepsi-Cola North America. He said I would work for him and focus on a situation that needed a great deal of clarity. The world of safety and risk management is fraught with complex laws and insurance actuarial red tape. Pepsi spent about $110 million annually to insure its thirty-five thousand employees and thirteen thousand vehicles, and the costs were rising rapidly. The job wasn't the prototypical human resources assignment, but I decided to "take one for the team" and agreed to the position as a springboard for other opportunities that would materialize down the road.

In just about a year, our team of very bright technical experts was able to reverse the cost trend, create a separate competition to highlight business performance by geography, and essentially make safety a priority for the company for the first time since I had been there. Before that, safety was something people talked about because it was politically correct to do so, but the programs were toothless—unable to impact the people they were designed to protect. During that year, though, we saved the company $10 million through safety initiatives.

Still, something was missing in my professional life. I wanted and needed more to fulfill my goals. In sports terms, I had been an assistant coach for eleven years and was itching to become a head coach. My career dream was to lead a major organization, first in human resources and then maybe in an operational role. I wanted to be responsible for making the calls, and I felt ready to do so. However, in a multi-billion-dollar company the road to the top is long, convoluted, and complicated. At another time I may have accepted a comfortable career, believing that my talent had taken me as far as I could go. I probably could have continued to thrive at Pepsi, but I also wanted to control my destiny. In my current role, and quite frankly in other roles I would play in successive assignments, I felt that too many other influences dictated the outcome of my livelihood, factors that would prevent me from having a major impact on the business for quite some time. My dream could have died, or at the very least hibernated, if my previous experiences had not taught me to think bigger. I committed myself to strive for something better.

Early in 1998, Dave Arnold, who had hired me at Pepsi back in 1987 but later left the company to become an executive recruiter at a search firm, called me about a different kind of assignment. His call made me reflect on our first meeting eleven years earlier. He had the boldness and the vision to take someone like me, with no formal human resources training, into an organization overflowing with top talent from the best HR schools in the country. I had kept in touch with Dave over the years, but this call was different than all the previous ones. I had been contacted about more senior HR roles many times, but none of them ever offered precisely what I wanted. Now Footstar, a company in New Jersey that had spun off from the Melville Corporation in 1996, was searching for its top human resources executive.

Since I had never spent any time in retail and didn't think it was an industry that would enhance my career goals, my initial reaction was lukewarm. Unfortunately, in an environment like Pepsi, it's easy to forget your roots and succumb to the arrogance that afflicts many successful people. I knew that in previous recruiter encounters I had displayed some of that arrogance, and I was determined not to allow that to happen again. What's more, I learned over time that it would be foolish not to listen, so I gave Dave the attentive respect due to someone in his position.

I didn't allow my initial misgivings to enter the discussion. Instead, I listened intently as Dave told me as much as he could about Footstar, an almost $2 billion retailer with fifteen thousand employees. At the same time, he managed my expectations. He said that he didn't know if I met the company's requirements since they had only interviewed sitting top HR executives up to that point. I'm not sure if he was looking for my gut reaction or for a crack in my confidence. I assured Dave that I felt ready for the challenge, and I offered some examples of how my experiences, though not aligning with all of Footstar's expectations, met the company's needs. In essence I told him, using the words of legendary lyricist John Fogerty of Creedence Clearwater Revival fame, "Put me in, Coach. I'm ready to play."[2]

Interviews were scheduled and information exchanged. The mating dance had begun and I thrust myself into the experience. The more I learned, the more excited I became. Footstar's leaders had aggressive plans for growth and development. After doing some research and consulting with friends, family, and professional contacts, all of my intellectual needs were satisfied. I became quite comfortable with the personal dynamics as well. On March 27, 1998, I received and accepted the offer to become, at the age of thirty-nine, the top HR professional in a publicly traded major corporation. I dared to dream and took the field.

---

2   "Centerfield." Lyrics and Music by John Fogerty. Album: *Centerfield*. 1985.

The story doesn't end there, however. After I had been the head of HR three years, the chairman approached me one day and asked if I wanted to lead the operations for a new acquisition the company had just made. The opportunity to run a business that was worth almost $300 million and included almost three thousand people would give me another chance to grow. I would also be able to apply many of the principles I had been preaching to other leaders throughout my career. Everything seemed destined for a happily-ever-after ending as I began that new chapter in my life on January 1, 2001.

Trouble in Paradise

But then a number of events merged and spoiled my fairy tale. Not long after the acquisition, several of the companies that Footstar had purchased the right to serve started to crumble. In many ways, capitalism worked as designed, as both Wal-Mart and Target moved into the Northeast markets, quickly siphoning business from two key regional chains, Caldor and Bradlees. They both filed for bankruptcy and soon liquidated their stores. Ames, another old Northeast commerce icon, along with its own miscalculated acquisition of Hills, also collapsed under the weight of Wal-Mart's might.

Kmart started to struggle again too. The chain that had dodged bankruptcy in the mid-nineties floundered under a new senior management team that was foolishly trying to copy Wal-Mart. Kmart decided to close several unprofitable stores, but it seemed to be too little too late. On September 11, 2001, Kmart was again teetering on the edge of bankruptcy because of additional business miscalculations.

The destruction of the World Trade Center's twin towers numbed the public's psyche, the American economy took a major body blow, and Kmart spiraled into bankruptcy, ultimately closing more than three hundred stores. A large percentage of Footstar's business was tied to Kmart and other licenses within stores that in a matter of months were out of business. The outcome was inevitable: Trouble with a capital T!

Almost overnight, Footstar's revenue stream fell far below the cost structure. The company was reeling, and in the process, personalities and biases were amplified. In an effort to stop the bleeding, budget cuts ensued. But nothing seemed to work. The perfect storm had unleashed every possible peril that could befall a company—all at the same time. Tension rose among the executive ranks as everyone hunkered down in survival mode.

There I was, a highly trained HR professional with little operations experience, running a business that was disintegrating before my eyes. Friction mounted between my boss and me as we worked to keep the ship afloat in a sea of red ink. Then I received the call that everyone dreads—I was out. Until that moment, the closest thing to feeling like a failure I had ever encountered was being benched when I played baseball at Navy. Like most people in that kind of situation, I was shocked. The company's difficulties were no longer a matter of professional survival. Maslow's hierarchy of needs kicked in—personal survival.

After experiencing a childhood of adversity and other trials throughout adulthood, I was struck with another potentially devastating blow. Everything I had worked to achieve was jeopardized, and all the hardship I thought I had overcome loomed over me again. God has a strange way of working, however. Just when I thought I had finally mastered the hitting game in corporate America, another curve ball came my way. Losing my job at Footstar was an additional test that further refined my character. After catching my breath, I developed a new game plan: pray, network, and sell my skills to whoever would listen. Those were trying days, but I had met numerous people and cultivated many friendships throughout my life. I contacted almost every one of them!

Fortunately, a new door opened for me at Home Depot not long after I started my search. There I gained more knowledge, developed more skills, and established even better friendships. Had I not accepted that job with Home Depot and moved to Atlanta, I likely wouldn't have received the opportunity to work for Starbucks, which then led to my current position as the chief people officer for Dollar General. I feel so fortunate to be part of this wonderful organization, a $16 billion company with more than ninety thousand employees in over ten thousand stores. And to think it all emerged from the ashes of yet more adversity.

From my trials over the years, I have learned about what was missing in my professional life. I have always worked hard, tried to do the right thing, and taken care of my family. I have also spent much of my past being too pragmatic and stuck in a quagmire of self-imposed limitations. I now know that dreams are vital to growth, success, and life. My dreams for the future are bright indeed. I expect to live many more years fulfilling my goals, especially giving back to society. More doors are open to me than ever before.

I have learned that I can accomplish anything if I invest the necessary amount of commitment, enthusiasm, and sacrifice. We can't limit ourselves by underestimating

our abilities or by listening to others who might do that
as well. Don't make the mistake I made early in life and
settle for anything less than what your heart and mind
are committed to achieving. One of the best attributes
of this country is the opportunity to excel, regardless of
circumstances or background. Go for it!

Reflection Questions

1. This chapter begins with the story of Wendy Lawrence,
    Bob's classmate at Navy. What is the closest you have
    come to establishing a long-term goal and then taking
    the necessary steps over time to pursue that goal?

2. Bob witnessed the launch of a space shuttle piloted
    by another Navy classmate, Brent Jett. Can you
    recall being inspired, or even overwhelmed, by
    the achievement of someone you know? Was that
    experience totally "sweet," or was it somewhat
    "bittersweet" because you wondered if that could have
    been your achievement?

3. Have you repressed a dream or aspiration because you
    thought it was beyond your reach?

4. Do you tend to struggle more with (a) pipe dreams—
    dreams that aren't based in reality and that you don't
    strive to make come true—or (b) being too pragmatic
    and stuck in a quagmire of self-imposed limitations?

5. If you could do anything in life, what would it
    be? Highly successful people put a portion of their
    downtime to work for them. Just two hours a week
    invested in your dream would create over a hundred

hours a year, or thirteen eight-hour days, to work toward that goal. What do you need to rearrange in your schedule so that you can pursue your dream?

Attitude Check

Change your thoughts and you change your world.
~ Norman Vincent Peale

At the end of the 1998 NFL football season, the St. Louis Rams were licking their wounds after finishing last in their division. Following his second losing season with the Rams, Coach Dick Vermeil's reputation as a winner was under intense scrutiny. The acquisition of talented running back Marshall Faulk in the off-season would likely add some punch to the offense, but no expert or knowledgeable fan expected him to be the answer to the Rams' problems. The 1999 preseason predictions indicated that the Rams would finish last in their division again.

When quarterback Trent Green suffered an injury in the preseason, the situation seemed to go from bad to worse. Enter an unknown former grocery store shelf-stocker named Kurt Warner, who had spent the beginning of the previous season in Europe before he became the Rams' third-string quarterback. In each of his first three starts of the 1999 season, Warner threw three touchdown passes, something that had never been done in the NFL. Then he threw five touchdown passes in the fourth game! Behind Warner's throwing arm and field leadership, the Rams not only won their division with a 13–3 record but also sailed through the playoffs and won the Super Bowl, a highly improbable feat. Warner won the MVP award for both the regular season and the Super Bowl, another spectacular accomplishment.

The sports world boasts a trophy case full of unlikely

turnarounds. Though comparable feats occur in other walks of life, they are less visible. A common attribute of these unexpected triumphs, however, regardless of the arena or the amount of attention, is enthusiasm.

Enthusiasm Is Contagious

All of us know people who are unpleasant to be around, often because of their values or attitudes. I have worked alongside a lot of people, and I have observed what causes some of them to end up on the wrong side of the success tracks. Those with poor values may succeed for a while, but they are eventually exposed. And those with negative attitudes are doomed from the beginning. What's more, they make life miserable for everyone around them. You know the type. The coworker who, when presented with an opportunity to lighten your load, always says no. The manager who gets up on the wrong side of the bed half the time and, unable to control his environment, takes it out on you. The relative who ruins every family get-together because she offends everyone there.

Regardless of our talents or opportunities, we increase our chances of success a hundredfold by having the right attitude. Think about what makes people successful. In politics, it's usually the candidate who paints the brightest picture of the future—leaders like John F. Kennedy and Ronald Reagan. Though many variables factored into the equation of their success, the fixed quantity was their positive impact on people. For Reagan, it was the portrait of America as a "shining city on a hill." JFK and his young family in the White House painted the image of an American Camelot, a vision of optimism and hope. Chuck

Swindoll, notable Christian leader and speaker, says this about attitude:

> The longer I live, the more I realize the impact of attitude on my life. Attitude, to me, is more important than facts. It is more important than the past, than education, than money, than circumstances, than failures, than successes, than what other people think or say or do. It is more important than appearance, giftedness, or skill. It will make or break a company, a church, or a home. The remarkable thing is that we have a choice every day regarding the attitude we will embrace for that day. We cannot change our past. Nor can we change the fact that people will act in a certain way. We also cannot change the inevitable. The only thing we can do is play on the one string we have, and that is our attitude. I am convinced that life is 10 percent what happens to me and 90 percent how I react to it. And so it is with you. We are in charge of our attitudes.[3]

People respond to positive enthusiasm. Mary Lou Retton remains memorable long after the Olympics in which she won a gold medal, whereas Mark Spitz, despite winning seven gold medals in one Olympics, never made much of a splash afterwards. While both dominated their sport at their respective Olympics, you might expect that Spitz, with his seven gold medals, would be in a league of his own in terms of fame and influence. Yet Retton is the one who conveys exuberance and garners attention. I could

---

3   Charles Swindoll. Quoted in Mac Anderson, *The Power of Attitude*. Nashville: Thomas Nelson, 2004. 110–11.

cite many other examples, but I'll use a personal one.

Throughout my youth, I tried to maintain an upbeat attitude. Maybe it was a defense mechanism to cover up the trouble at home, including the lack of a positive father in my life. Or perhaps, since we moved so often, it was my way of ensuring I could adapt to my new surroundings more easily. Whatever the reason, I remained upbeat—which made me more outgoing, which in turn made people want to be around me. I also noticed that I wanted to be around others with an outgoing personality and an optimistic view of the world. Friends came easily, teachers enjoyed having me in class, and coaches liked instructing me. Attitude is one of those "intangibles" coaches often mention. Teachers like students who have a positive attitude because they deal with so many students who are negative. A positive attitude is both magnetic and contagious.

Overcoming Obstacles

People with a positive mindset encounter plenty of obstacles, however. For example, I had a head on collision with failure when I lost my starting position on the Navy baseball team. But it became a pivotal point in my life.

Following my sophomore year, in which I was the youngest starter on the team, I was sitting on top of the world. I had gotten my break when John Zaccardi, the previous starting first baseman, who was a year ahead of me, left the Academy after signing a pro contract with the San Francisco Giants. John was a great ballplayer, so who knows what my chances would have been had he remained with the team. Needless to say, I was in the right place at the right time. In retrospect, though, I let my status go to my head. After the season ended, I did very little to keep in shape. Why should I? I had started the previous year on a championship team, and I saw no prospects that could beat me out in the next two years. Or so I thought. Though not a conscious choice on my part, what befell me that summer of 1979 was overconfidence, a weakness that often leads to arrogance. Fortunately, I learned a valuable life lesson from it.

While other college ballplayers were spending the summer honing their skills, my teammates and I took to the fleet for our required military training, beginning with a four-week rotation between the Marines, Navy air, submarines, and surface line. Another few weeks were spent back at the Academy for additional military training. We were left with only a few short weeks of downtime before the fall semester, of which I took full advantage.

Throughout the fall season I felt like the team and our skills progressed as usual, but I sensed that Coach Duff saw me in a somewhat different light. Maybe my attitude was different. Maybe I was performing like I had a lock on my position. Whatever it was, he rode me pretty hard. On the annual early spring trip to play the powerful Louisiana and Mississippi teams, I played every day, but I wasn't getting the hits or making the progress I expected. By the end of the trip, I didn't feel great about my readiness. Still I looked forward to the regular season beginning back home.

I'll never forget what happened next. Going into our first regular season home game, I thought I would finally put it all together. Except for one thing. During warm-ups Coach Duff called me aside and in a stark, cold, and piercing voice told me he was pulling me from the lineup and inserting in my place a sophomore who had played on the junior varsity team the previous year. He gave no further explanation. I was stunned! If you've ever had the wind knocked out of you from an unexpected blow to the midsection, you know how I felt.

Before each game the starters took batting practice as a unit, so I was now banished to the field for batting practice. More disgrace. And rather than sitting in the dugout during the game I would be dispatched to the bullpen, where everyone but the starters sat until they were called for duty—if they ever were called. More indignity. So on top of the knockout blow, I had to face the humiliation in front of the rest of the team. Almost immediately there were looks and questions from my teammates. Devastated and embarrassed, I sulked. And shortly thereafter, I yielded to anger.

Needless to say, I didn't handle my new status very well. I complained about the coach's decision and wallowed in self-pity. I had arrived at a critical crossroad in my baseball career. Though the whole season was in front of us, I assumed I was banished to the bullpen for the duration. I had two choices: I could quit or I could suck it up and do my best. And if I didn't quit, I would eventually have to assess my status for my senior year.

I decided to stick it out and contribute any way I could. Every day at practice I worked to improve my game, even staying afterward to get in extra swings and to field ground balls. The season proved to be tough for both me personally and the team—we finished second in our league and lost to Army for the first time in years. We ended the season with a 22–6 record but fell one game short of the league championship. I appeared in twenty-three of the games, though in a limited capacity, and hit .368.

After that it was decision time. I had invested a great

deal of time and energy during the previous three years, which forced me to answer a difficult question: did I want to play baseball one more year with no guarantee of additional playing time?

Never Give Up

I examined my options long and hard. I asked key people in my life for advice. Just before the end of my summer cruise in the Mediterranean on board the USS *Saratoga*, I decided to give it my all for the final year. I wasn't sure how much I was going to play, but baseball had helped me get into the Academy and I wasn't one to quit—at anything. I practiced after the cruise, came back in the best shape in my life, and played every inning of every game in 1981, finishing with a .340 average and becoming an honorable mention all-league selection. At the end of the season, I was glad that I had stuck with the program and finished on a high note. I still consider that season one of the greatest achievements of my life.

I have carried a never-give-up mindset throughout my life, and I have also come to realize that the concept transcends age. While coaching my daughter Cryssa's fourth-grade basketball team, I was looking for an edge against an overpowering opponent. You might be surprised to learn that girls at that age can be very competitive, especially in a league that created an aura of competition with its standings and playoffs. My girls really wanted to win, and from the beginning I preached a positive attitude and did little things to pump them up. I called out specific individuals when they made a good play. I also reminded them that few teams ever achieve greatness, but they had a

chance to do just that. It's amazing what a little praise can
do or the prospect of accomplishing something special can
achieve, even for a bright-eyed group of nine- to ten-year-
olds. I had learned that the simpler you keep things, at any
level, the better the performance. Usually it comes down
to execution. Using that philosophy, we won our first eight
games.

But then the girls went up against another 8–0 team.
And I knew, from watching some of the opponent's
games, that they had more skilled players at every position,
including a girl named Abby Waner. She later led her high
school team to three state titles, became the Gatorade
High School National Player of the Year, McDonald's
high school All-American, a standout player at Duke, and
eventually played for the New York Liberty in the WNBA.
Even when she was a fourth grader, anyone could tell that
she had extraordinary skills. And she wasn't even the best
kid on that team.

Nonetheless, I coached the girls to work hard, run the
plays, and have confidence—to believe that they could beat
that team. In the first quarter, a real defensive struggle,
we held our own. But although we held a 6–4 lead after
the quarter, I sensed in the huddle that the girls didn't
realize they had outplayed their opponents for six minutes.
They just needed to keep doing it for the rest of the game.
Unfortunately, the other team scored a few quick baskets to
take the lead, and then went on to rout my girls by a final
score of 24–8. A blowout!

What had gone wrong? Part of the carnage was my
fault. I didn't have an effective defensive strategy. Abby
Waner's eight points and Kristen Van's twelve points
constituted twenty of the team's twenty-four points. When
that wrecking crew wasn't scoring, they were grabbing

rebounds and leading fast breaks. On the other hand, nothing we did worked. We scored only two more points after the first quarter.

When we played our nemesis again later in the season, our team still only had one loss and they were still undefeated. After giving careful thought to my strategy, I explained it to my eldest daughter, Cryssa, the night before the game. She looked at me inquisitively since I had a big grin on my face. If my daughter is anything, she is tenacious. Though she was one of our leading scorers, I had made a rather unusual decision. I knew we wouldn't be able to outgun the opponent and win the battle by trading baskets. I needed another plan, and I divulged it to Cryssa.

I was going to use Cryssa in a one-on-one match-up with their best player, the one who had sunk twelve against us earlier. Our other defensive stand out, Carrie Hickey, would block Waner, the future WNBA player. I told Cryssa that her job would be to prevent that girl from touching the ball. When we had the ball, Cryssa would stay out of the flow, standing near half court, for two reasons. First, man-to-man rules in the league required every girl to stay on an opposing player. Second, many of the baskets scored against us in the first game were fast-break lay-ups, easy buckets. To round out the strategy, the rest of the team would play four-on-four.

Before the game, I laid out my strategy in the huddle. The girls cheered enthusiastically as they headed out to the floor. When the final whistle blew, the girls had done it—prevailing 17–16! They maintained the right mental attitude to pull off a tremendous upset against a team that didn't lose another game all season and easily won the championship. I was so proud of the girls. Cryssa had sacrificed her role on offense for the good of the team and held Van, the opposition's high-scorer, to zero points. Hickey not only held Waner in check, but she also scored seven points, including the game winning free throws with four seconds remaining. Most fulfilling for me, however, was the badge of confidence each girl had won, medallions they wore for many years to come. Their attitude made the difference that day. Every event—even for a fourth grader—can teach a lesson that lasts a lifetime.

No Room for Negative Waves

No one enjoys what Donald Sutherland's character, Oddball, in the movie *Kelly's Heroes*, aptly referred to as "negative waves."[4] Evidently, many people don't understand Oddball's point, though, because I have seen so many get derailed by a negative attitude. Several of my teammates were never able to show what they could do because their attitude either prompted the coach to cut them or they became so frustrated that they quit.

By far, the most significant issue in every organization I have been associated with has been attitude. When the attitude was positive, teams, departments, and the organization as a whole flourished. When the attitude was negative, every entity invariably fell short of their objectives. Changing a culture is tough, but often it's only the perception of the environment that needs to change.

When I began working for Footstar, one of my initial priorities was to conduct an employee attitude survey because it effectively measures an organization's vital

---

4   *Kelly's Heroes*. Produced by Gabriel Katzka, Harold Loeb, and Sidney Beckerman. Directed by Brian G. Hutton. Metro-Goldwyn-Mayer. 1970.

signs. At the same time we established an environment committee, made up of about ten individuals who represented a cross section of the company. An interesting dynamic emerged as these concurrent processes were underway. Some people were skeptical of our motives, and some intuitively felt that the company didn't support an environment friendly to individuals. Ironically, when the scores were calculated, the company actually did better than expected, surpassing national norms in several categories. Yet some members of the committee felt that people were constrained by the environment. Rather than telling them to suck it up, I decided to coach them on how to overcome perceived constraints. Incidentally, the committee recommended several key initiatives that were implemented in the company. They took the opportunity to make a difference, focusing on the possibilities rather than the barriers.

At Pepsi, I worked with one person who was very negative—an anomaly in the company. To this day I'm amazed he survived so long in an environment that bleeds positive energy and enthusiasm. Sometimes organizations overlook shortcomings for the sake of hitting the bottom line. As I worked with this fellow, attended meetings with him, and listened to subordinates complain about him, it became evident that I needed to talk to him about his attitude. When I confronted him, he shifted the blame: his team whined about him, he didn't have enough resources to do his job, and others singled him out because he didn't "kiss ass" or fall in line. Unfortunately, he missed the point . . . and the next paycheck. His negativity cost him his job.

A positive attitude also promotes better health. You've probably heard that it takes more muscles to frown than to smile. It also takes a lot more energy to cope with stress or depression, which both impede performance. I have been on the wrong side of the "fortunate tracks" many times. Each time I had to decide whether I would allow the situation to pull me into the abyss of despair or fight it and break its corrosive chains.

Positive Mojo

My daughter Katie exudes positive waves. Every morning she wakes up with a smile. She has always been friendly and, as a result, popular in school. Two weeks after she entered fifth grade at a new school, Katie hosted a sleepover for every girl in her class. They all wanted to be there. She played in five championship games by the time she was ten, due in great part to the optimistic attitude she and her teammates exhibited. In high school, her team skills made her a cherished member of the volleyball team. Now a college graduate, Katie fully understands the impact of her attitude—and she's like a magnet.

My son Brett, who graduated from high school in 2012, is also a very good athlete. But he is too hard on himself. I've coached a lot of teams over the years, and I know how critical a short memory is, whether you've just made a good play or a bad play. Brett overanalyzes his challenges, so I constantly have to encourage him with positive self-talk. For example, in youth baseball he hit over .600 and over .500 in successive seasons, yet he repeatedly focused on the occasional strikeout or fly-out. He was so afraid of swinging and missing or making an out that he would take good pitches. I must have told him a thousand times, "You can't get a hit if you don't swing." I finally advised him to swing at anything he could get his bat on, even if he struck out every time. Just swing. Once Brett got comfortable with that philosophy he began to hit everything in sight, which built his confidence. That, in turn, led to even more success, which ultimately led to him signing an offer to play baseball in college. Now he accepts positive reinforcement and lets go of mistakes. For Brett, the best is yet to come.

Everyone faces trying circumstances. I overcame an anxiety-filled childhood afflicted by poverty and my father's alcoholism. I constantly felt the stress of trying to excel both academically and athletically. Later, I contended with the relentless barrage of upperclassmen tirades at the Naval Academy. In adulthood I've encountered a multitude of recurring stress points, the kind that trouble everyone from time to time.

Fortunately, I've been able to hurdle these obstacles—to master the little stresses before they become big ones. Something that often helps me during low points is to focus on people who are facing much more difficult circumstances than I am. It's hard to feel sorry for myself when I'm thinking about someone who is dealing with a great challenge or a deep loss. I highly recommend the *Chicken Soup for the Soul* series of books, which are filled with anecdotes that not only bring tears to my eyes but also remind me that every person in the world matters. I am also inspired by reading the Bible, especially its stories and psalms, because doing so helps me remember that God has a purpose for my feelings and my future. We are indeed blessed with access to an unlimited library that can assist us in getting over the blues and developing a healthier outlook on life.

As I take these steps, I stop stewing over my own troubles and soon reverse the downward spiral. What

works for me may not work for you. My point is that each
of us holds the key that unlocks the door to a positive
attitude. Find the right door, overcome your fears, and
use that key. Medical experts continually warn us about
the detriments of a poor attitude, beginning perhaps with
stress-related heart attacks and followed by many other
ailments, some of which may be life threatening. We are
what we make of ourselves, and we have the power to
improve our lives.

In my professional role, employees commonly ask me
how they can advance in our company. The first thing I
say is that they've already taken the first step by asking.
Much of the rest is up to them. How they perform in
their current role obviously plays a huge part in their
future. And attitude has a lot to do with performance. Too
often employees want the benefits of a promotion—pay,
perks, status—but are unwilling to take the steps to get
there. Many people assume their company owes them
a promotion based on seniority alone. The two things
a company owes its workers are a safe environment free
from hostility and a steady paycheck for meeting the
requirements of their job. Nothing else! Any other gain
that comes their way, in large part, hinges on them.

Another Mountain to Climb

I like to jog, but it wasn't until I started using a portable
music device that jogging became tolerable. I often listened
to audio books or motivational speakers, which pushed
me to earn an MBA and kept me energized through all the
projects, papers, and finals. One speaker began with a story
about a concert pianist playing at the hallowed Carnegie

demands, so with every step up in the company I took, my duties increased. In addition, as a field human resources director, I was on the road almost every week for several days at a time. Routines go to hell when you're on the road, so in addition to losing the luxury of my office, managing my time became more difficult.

Perhaps you're thinking, *Okay, as busy as I am already, how do I stay on top of my workload and achieve the kind of work/life balance that I want and need?* Well, there is no magic formula, but here are a few key principles that have helped me.

Principle 1: Practice finish-line thinking

Just as many people live paycheck to paycheck financially, they also approach life in general the same way: day to day. Successful people adopt finish-line thinking. They know what they want to accomplish, design a game plan to achieve it, and execute that plan to completion. Everything they do is geared toward reaching that goal. Countless numbers of people with excellent ideas start projects but never finish them. Before any of the other principles will help you, you need to map out *how* you're going to move forward.

So many people take one step and then take the next step based on what transpired. In other words, they use a very reactionary approach to whatever they are doing. We all have to adjust to changing circumstances, but if we don't know our destination, we'll probably travel in endless circles.

When I joined Dollar General, the company had no human resources strategy, so the team was caught in a perpetual cycle of responding to the requests that were thrust upon them. As a result, the work may have been completed, but the discussion was one-sided—from the business leaders to the HR community. I knew that our team needed to develop a strategy that would enable the company to become an employer of choice, with a long-range plan. Consequently, everyone would understand the process, buy in, and help us achieve our shared goals.

Principle 2: Remove the clutter from your mind

Both the desire to perform and the ability to achieve spring from sound mental health. A healthy mind is like a well-oiled machine. And the healthiest state of mind is driven by being present in the moment—or, as it is often called, being in the zone. The zone is that place of rarefied air where the mind is clear to focus only on the immediate moment. Athletes and coaches often speak of this realm where nothing interferes with their task. But guess what? The zone isn't reserved for athletes only. Everyone performs better when they can get in the zone. The determining factor is your ability to remove all the external influences and distractions from your mind and function solely through internal means.

Many people are driven by what others think or say about them. Or their own self-doubts about their abilities immobilize them. Some won't even make a decision for fear of making a mistake, particularly in relation to how those around them might be affected. Unfortunately, many people's minds are cluttered with this kind of garbage. The voices that help you get in the zone are whispers, constantly trying to overcome the external clutter, which blares like a brass band. No wonder so few achieve this state of well-being and that those who do are exceptional talents! The good news is that everyone can learn to unclutter their minds, but only a precious few are willing to invest the time necessary to master it.

The final spoke in the wheel is who, or what, helps you focus on the internal forces and drive away the external ones. For employees, that takes the form—hopefully—of their immediate supervisor or coach. Think for a moment about how significant supervisors can be to the individuals entrusted to their care. Good supervisors help new employees feel welcome in the company, provide positive coaching, give them the proper tools to do their job, and then get out of their way. From a professional standpoint, that process helps employees build self-confidence and feel good about their contribution. It also removes the barriers that prohibit them from getting into the zone, and it spurs them toward peak performance. On the other hand, poor supervisors can unravel employees, undermining their self-esteem and accomplishments, which, in turn, prevents them from reaching their potential.

Personal issues are often more difficult to manage than professional issues; however, we can often control our own destiny in private matters. Everyone faces challenges from time to time: money problems, family issues, or work-related stress. Whatever the cause, the principles still apply. To be successful in any endeavor or area, you must achieve that healthy mental state.

What's amazing about the zone is that success feeds on itself. Focus on one thing at a time, accomplish it, and then move on to the next item.

Principle 3: Plan everything and write it all down

I have worked with many brilliant people over the years, and the ones who have distinguished themselves by finishing the job weren't those who prided themselves on their memory and therefore refused to write things down. No, those who are successful are the ones who realize that they can't remember everything. The adage that advises "the devil is in the details" is particularly applicable to successfully completing a project.

Think of your own life. How often do you forget to write something down or write it on the first piece of scrap paper you find and then misplace it? Consider the countless hours you have wasted trying to track down information that should have been safely recorded. Inaccessible or forgotten information is a daily frustration for a lot of people, and something I had to overcome as well.

The daily regimen at the Naval Academy was my first formal exposure to scheduling. From reveille at dawn until taps (lights out) late at night, my day was planned: breakfast to classes to lunch to classes to baseball practice to dinner to studying. We were all given daily calendars to use, but much of the time I winged it. The biggest challenge was budgeting the limited free time we were allocated. With six classes to study for and with professors that often scheduled tests in the same week, budgeting study time was critical. I didn't manage my time as well as I should have, and I often spent too much time on one thing and not enough on another.

Once I was in the fleet, managing a host of people

and equipment, winging it became much tougher. With so many issues to address, I began to carry a little pocket notebook in an effort to keep all the data straight in my head. Even in its most rudimentary stages, that written record made it easier to manage my day. The key was that all the information was in one location, so that even if I couldn't remember a specific task or status, I only needed to look in one place to find it.

Not until I joined the corporate sector, however, did I fully appreciate the need to be organized. Coming into Pepsi's environment was like going from a slow run on a treadmill to a life-and-death flight from an oncoming train. Knowing that if I didn't stay in front of it the train would run me over, I became serious about organization. The first step was developing a plan, which included writing everything down. I also attended a time management seminar soon after I began to work for Pepsi. That seminar, with its emphasis on the daily planner concept, changed the way I approached my daily life.

As an example, while in my first position in human resources at Pepsi, I arrived at the office at 5:30 a.m. to conduct a roundtable discussion with several hourly and commissioned employees. At 6:30 a.m. I walked the floor of the plant, talking to other employees and often speaking to a manager or two about emerging employee issues or upcoming job openings. Then I went to my office to sift through a stack of résumés while I answered voice mails. The day might also have included an unemployment hearing, an OSHA inspection, or a union contract negotiation, and I always had to allow prep time for those events. Cyclical processes occur throughout the year, so I might have spent the balance of the morning preparing wage and benefit summaries. Each moment of the day I

was either giving or receiving information, all of which had
to be written down or it might be lost.

I usually ate lunch at my desk while I answered more
voice mails; fortunately, email has significantly reduced
phone time. Several messages each day required follow-
up, which needed to be written down as well. Sometimes
I had to draft a memo on a policy issue and then attend a
staff meeting to get the latest updates on the state of the
business. I also had to visit other sites, which required
travel time for scheduled meetings with key people. Other
days included a dinner activity with an employment
candidate or colleague before I could go home to unwind.

Obviously, every day didn't require fourteen to sixteen
hours, but ten to twelve hours was the norm, plus time on
the weekends. I discovered, very early in my career, that I
could easily get swallowed up by the job if I didn't keep a
record of everything I needed to get done and the progress
I was making toward that end. In order to retain my sanity,
I needed to coordinate and schedule my day to maximize
effectiveness. I've been able to juggle a lot of balls at one
time as well as meet deadlines and obligations because I
habitually plan my schedule and write it all down.

When was the last time you scheduled a one-hour
workout into your day? How often do you put your
child's soccer game in your day planner? Too often these
personal events are ignored because we separate them from
the business day. Planning and writing down our *entire*
schedule ensures that we don't miss important personal
events. I wouldn't have been able to coach over fifty youth
teams unless I had command of my schedule.

Principle 4: Get into a routine and stick to it

Every day when I come home from work, I place my car keys on their assigned hook, put my wallet in its place, change my clothes, and then select my attire for the next day. Routines, including using a daily planner and always having a notepad or smartphone handy, make life much more manageable.

How often have you been unable to find something in your house? That used to happen to me all the time until I established the routine of putting things in the same place all the time. Likewise, I infuse as much routine into my workday as possible. For instance, rather than taking every phone call, I generally let incoming calls go into voice mail and then answer them at two intervals, once in the morning and once near the end of the day.

Some of this advice may sound so simple that you wonder how much difference it can make. In and of themselves these routines may not amount to much, but combined they represent a significant difference between the healthiest state of mind and something less than that. Take sleep, for example. I try to go to bed and get up at the same time on weekends as I do during the week. Why? It isn't a coincidence that Mondays are so hard on people. They change their routine on the weekend and pay the price on Monday. If I am disciplined enough to stay in my routine over the weekend, Monday morning feels like any other morning. Some might argue that such a regimen drains all the fun and spontaneity out of life. All I know is that I feel much better *in* my routine than *out* of it.

What's more, disciplines and routines only bind us when we lack the commitment or conviction to stick

to them. I have known many people who entered a
family event in their day planners only to rearrange their
schedules at the first sign of conflict. These same people
may not think twice about being late for a meeting with a
subordinate or peer, but they bend over backwards to get
to a meeting early with someone senior.

I treat each event on my schedule with equal
importance. Part of our long-term success in life is
building credibility among the people we associate with,
including family, friends, coworkers, and clients. None of
them should be sacrificed for something or someone we
perceive to be more important. Occasionally, a conflict
is unavoidable. However, if you have earned a level of
credibility with the people involved, they'll be more likely
to understand.

When I was working as a junior HR manager in
1988, a significant part of my job involved interacting
with employees. Before leaving the office at the end of
each day, I called my wife, Lisa, trying to be sensitive to
her schedule, to tell her I was heading home for dinner.
As I walked through the building, invariably an employee,
supervisor, or plant manager wanted to discuss some
issue. Because I didn't want to appear insensitive to their
concerns, I stopped and listened. Unfortunately, one-
minute conversations occasionally extended to thirty
minutes or longer. Sometimes I called Lisa again and
sometimes I didn't. Eventually, she became very upset
with me because I was being inconsiderate and making
her feel as if she wasn't important. The issue wasn't the
time I was coming home, but my bad habit of breaking a
commitment I had made. Lisa was open enough to share
her frustration with me, and today I am quite cognizant of
the commitments I make to her and to anyone else.

Maybe you need the same message. I challenge you to be a person of conviction. If you have something planned and your manager needs you to stay late, let them know about your conflict. If they insist you stay, that company probably isn't worth working for. What's more, the extent to which your personal and family life is balanced will factor into your performance on the job.

I define a balanced life much differently than many other people do. So I intentionally discuss work and family balance with my staff. At Pepsi, I created a goal sheet that I asked all of my staff to complete. A few years ago, a staff member stated on his goal sheet that his request for balance was to use his three weeks of vacation during the year. I was astounded by his comment because that was something he was already entitled to as an employee. Vacation time is meant to be used, yet this employee hadn't taken a vacation for several years. I challenged him to manage his work time more efficiently, and I promised that I wouldn't intervene and cancel any of his vacation time.

A clear way to avoid most uncomfortable situations is to give your boss a schedule of your personal activities and vacation in advance, thus eliminating any surprises. Managers are responsible to plan according to the resources at their disposal. It's also important for employees to stick to their convictions and not cave in at the first sign that someone needs them. No doubt employees will encounter circumstances in which they'll feel unbalanced. After challenging the status quo and giving a manager notice, employees may then be forced into a lifestyle decision if they feel like they can't accomplish their goals at that company.

Managers must also realize that people won't stay long at a place where their perceived rights are trampled.

I have never canceled someone's vacation, and I can't see an instance where I would ever have to do that, except in the most extreme emergency. Putting an employee in that predicament is a result of poor planning and an inability to manage resources well.

Principle 5: Move out of your comfort zone

Returning home after my first semester at the Naval Academy, I discovered that I had grown more intellectually and emotionally than I had realized. I was much more responsible, reflective, and emotionally mature than I had been six months earlier. Many of my friends were also in their first year of college, but our respective regimens were vastly different. To put it in perspective, while the average college freshman was taking twelve credits, I was taking twenty-one. While the average freshman's first class started in the middle of the morning, my days began at 5:30 a.m. And I had been immersed in my collegiate environment all summer while my buddies were still partying. Even after their semester began, they were listening to their stereos and watching TV almost every night. I, on the other hand, had no access to radio or TV and couldn't speak to anyone outside my room.

You've likely heard that what doesn't kill you makes you stronger. Well, I became stronger real fast as a midshipman. In part, it was a matter of survival. But more importantly, for the first time in my life, I was pushed far beyond my comfort zone. And although it was painful at times, that plebe year at the Academy was instrumental in molding me into the person I am today. I have stretched my horizons and tried new things. Going into the submarine force, the most challenging of the services, was no mistake either. And making the jump from the Navy to the corporate world also forced me to leave my comfort zone for an unknown fate. Many make the military a career because they love it, but some stay in it for the security of retirement it provides.

I have exposed myself to forced growth many times over the last thirty years—including some of the opportunities I've pursued outside of work, like becoming a youth league head coach, starting a high school alumni association, and teaching Sunday school when my knowledge of the Bible was minimal. It's hard for me to imagine living my life any other way. All these experiences shoved me out of my comfort zone, and I have benefited from every one of them.

Coming from the military, where rank is revered, I had difficulty adapting to the corporate environment where everyone is on a first-name basis. Approaching a senior officer uninvited was almost unheard of when I was in the service, but in the corporate world it is a sign of strength. During my early days at Pepsi, I struggled with that mindset. Then I received some great advice from Terry Kirby, the vice president of human resources for the eastern United States. He encouraged me to contact the senior vice president of HR every six to twelve months and invite him to lunch. Though Terry recommended that I always have an agenda, he said that initiating such a meeting, most importantly, would show my comfort level in the senior VP's presence. It would also give me the opportunity to get some one-on-one time that is both valuable and hard to obtain. Well, it worked. Since then I have grown quite comfortable around the most senior people and no longer hesitate to mingle in those circles.

Another worthwhile way to move out of your comfort zone is to volunteer for things outside your realm of expertise. Whether on the job or in your personal life, volunteering is an effective way to learn new skills, to be recognized for your efforts, and to gain an added measure of satisfaction—all of which build self-confidence. When a project came along, I invariably volunteered because it usually had national implications, enabled me to meet and work with others I may not have otherwise encountered, and expanded my horizons. Volunteering has no downside if you manage it well: it improves your ability to juggle more balls, increases your overall performance, and enhances your value to any organization.

Learning new information or technology is another way to stretch yourself. Going to night school for three and a half years wasn't fun; however, getting an MBA expanded my knowledge base and forced me to manage my time better. I was also able to network with other professionals from an array of backgrounds and take an arsenal of new ideas back to my job.

Which direction will you take in your life—the easier, more traveled path, or the path that leads you outside your comfort zone? You have every reason to believe you will be happy and satisfied on the first path. Take the latter one, however, and I guarantee you will feel much more alive and in control of your life. Push yourself to new heights. Not only will you like the panoramic view, you will also gain a whole new zest for life.

Reflection Questions

1. All of us struggle to keep our minds uncluttered. What distractions or interests tend to hinder your focus? In what way(s) do you need to move out of your comfort zone? What step(s) will you take to do so?

2. What does it mean to practice "finish-line thinking"? Do you practice that mental discipline or do you usually just wing it?

3. When have you felt that you were "in the zone"? What circumstances contributed to making that happen? What steps would help you get in the zone more often?

4. To what extent do you have a routine—and stick to it? How hard is it for you to stand your ground when professional pressures threaten your personal and family life?

5. Do you treat each event and person on your schedule as no less important than any other? How could you grow in that regard?

6. For one week, record your entire schedule—every activity. Then analyze how you spent your time. Look for ways you can maximize your productivity, such as streamlining scattered tasks—e.g., creating periodic slots each day to respond to e-mails and calls. Next, as much as possible, plan and write down your intended complete schedule for one week. Reflect afterwards on what you learned and on what you want to incorporate permanently from this exercise.

7. In what way(s) do you need to move out of your comfort zone? What step(s) will you take to do so?

Glance Backward, Then Move Forward

One man with courage is a majority.
~Andrew Jackson

I've probably passed the halfway point in my life, and so far it's been quite a ride. With so much more to learn and do, I believe the best years are still ahead. I wake up every morning looking forward to trying something new. That excitement fuels my drive. From my drive come ideas. From my ideas come possibilities. And from possibilities comes reality. What better way to live?

Obviously, though, I haven't always lived that way. I have suffered through tremendous pain and many sleepless nights to get to a better place in my head and in my heart. Sometimes the pain seemed unbearable. Other people, who have lived through similar experiences, have probably felt like that, too. At one point, I articulated the pain in rhymed verse, attempting to visualize it and to aid the healing process:

Pain

God created it or so it seems
To remind us who's mortal, who controls all the dreams
You can't hide from it, try to run if you dare
It's certain to catch you—where? It doesn't care

It has chained me, I've been shackled much of my life
As a child, at home, alone with my strife

I have tried to fight, defended my best
But it finds a way, to add another test

Nowhere to turn, will it ever go away?
What will work? I tried laughter today
I thought my life full, wife and kids were my pride
But my God only knows, part of me already died

What keeps me going, I cannot say
Only hope, and love, and the capacity to pray
And life must go on, I push myself to the brink
For that day it's no more, it allows me to think

I need to hold on, no one must see
Push the darkness away, till the sun shines on me
When will it end? Must find strength and compete
To cherish my family, my wife, all so sweet

And cast it aside like so many times before
Beat it back to its cavern, so deep in my core
But knowing full well, it only hibernates
Till someone or something, alters its fate

So I must respect its power, its disabling sound
So I can control it, not the other way around

Converting my pain into positive energy was an arduous
process, which demanded a resolute will and unwavering
persistence. I'm not sure when my determination to excel
began, but I'm sure glad it did. I've been influenced by so
many good people and have experienced so many great
things that I can't begin to repay all the good that has come
my way nor completely describe all the lessons I've learned

along the journey. I'd like to think, though, that learning how to respond to my circumstances has ultimately been the greatest lesson of all.

You may be wondering what happened to my dysfunctional, self-destructing family. My parents divorced in 1978 and went their separate ways. One night in 1986 a ringing telephone awoke me. Someone from the sheriff's office in St. Petersburg, Florida, was calling to tell me that my father had been found dead in his apartment, apparently of natural causes. He was sixty-four. Unfortunately, he had lost touch with his family and ultimately lost his battle with alcohol. After I entered the Academy in 1977, our contact had been very limited. Despite all the pain and suffering Dad had brought into my life, I still felt that he should attend my graduation in 1981, so I paid for his bus ticket. Though he had really deteriorated by that time, he made it through the ceremony. Observing the pride on his face as he looked at me outfitted in my dress whites, I knew he was happy.

He also made it to my wedding on July 7, 1982, haggard and sallow. At least he was able to stand and take a photo with me, in my Navy Dinner Dress Blue uniform, and with his brother Jay, who had followed him while growing up but watched in anguish as alcohol destroyed Dad's life. It was a bittersweet moment. Dad looked as good as he could in a tuxedo for the event, but it was also the last time I saw my dad standing on his own.

Early in 1984, while waiting to board our submarine crew's overseas flight, I was stopped at the gate and told that my father was near death. I immediately flew to Florida and spent several days, along with my younger brother, Greg, watching over Dad in a veteran's hospital bed. He had brief periods of consciousness, and he smiled when he eventually recognized my face, but I thought it was clearly the end for him. Emaciated and semiconscious, he looked terrible. It was painful to watch him go through that kind of suffering. A few moments of hope and conversation punctuated our vigil, but mostly my brother and I just held Dad's hand.

Miraculously, Dad recovered enough to be released from the hospital. But the war with the bottle that he had waged all his life finally conquered him two years later. We buried him in the national cemetery at Pinelawn, New York. Ironically, my maternal grandfather had also been interred there. I couldn't ignore the contrast between those two men or the vastly different impact they both had on my life.

My mother also died in Florida, in 2006, with my youngest sister, Diann, at her side. She didn't get around much toward the end of her life, but she was still as tough as a horse, even though she battled cancer three times before it defeated her. Although many years of strife had embittered her, and the relationship between her and me was often strained, Mom's last bout with the dreaded disease softened her a great deal. Some of the discord was rooted in the past. I clung to the belief that she could have pulled her children out of that corrosive environment long before she finally did. From my earliest recollections until I left for the Academy at eighteen, life at home was unbearable. For whatever reason, maybe an unwillingness to take a risk, Mom languished not only in a failed marriage but also in a sea of self-pity and abuse. Fortunately, God answered my prayers and eased my pain so that I no longer feel any bitterness toward her. Neither do I blame her for all that my siblings and I endured. It was an oppressive burden, but I ultimately laid it down and made my peace with my mother before she passed.

My siblings have moved on to what would appear to be normal everyday lives to the casual observer. Look a little deeper, though, and you will realize that each of us has been significantly scarred by our upbringing. Our families have little meaningful contact. I suppose we all have demons to battle and are haunted by past trauma. The search for peace and tranquility may be a lifelong quest. Because my childhood memories are painful, my defense mechanism is to push those memories into the far corners of my mind. The truly unfortunate aftermath is that the earlier challenges still affect my siblings and me, although we continue to function in our respective worlds. Fortunately, the past has not repeated itself in the next generation—a tribute to the willpower of my brothers and sisters.

At the very least, our childhood experiences taught us to never put our families through anything like the perpetual nightmare we survived. And my own vast supply of imperfections humbles me whenever I get cocky. I struggle as much as anyone else with the execution of all the good advice that crosses my path. I'm not perfect, but I've learned not to beat myself up over it.

Make a Difference

Life happens. The question is, what are you going to do about it? Don't sit on the sidelines and watch life pass by. Being a spectator often leads to bitterness, envy, and cynicism. Don't end up like that. A clever American proverb says there are three types of people: those who make things happen, those who watch things happen, and those who don't know what's happening! Which category are you in?

Hope is not a strategy, but you need hope to build a life strategy. You make choices every day. Many people around you can give you hope. Look for them, invite them into your life, and then commit yourself to excellence. Make a difference in your life and in the lives of others. You'll be much happier because of it.

Embrace risk. Nothing stands in your way but your own constraints. I have learned the most by venturing into territory where I felt the least comfortable. Nothing in life is guaranteed, and nothing worthwhile will ever be easy. But with the right attitude, aptitude, and aspiration, you can live a more fulfilled and more successful life. You can make significant progress and positive change if you implement the principles I've outlined in this book.

Do you dream of scaling the peaks of success? Do you long to see the view from the summit? Turn your dream into reality. Get up. Step up. Stay up. The difference between today and tomorrow is you.

About the Author

Bob Ravener currently serves as the Executive Vice President and Chief People Officer for the **Dollar General Corporation**, a Fortune 200 publicly traded company. In this capacity, Mr. Ravener has leadership responsibility for all Human Resources initiatives for a $16+ billion company with more than 90,000 employees in over 10,500 stores.

Prior to joining Dollar General, Mr. Ravener was Senior Vice President US Partner Resources, for the **Starbucks Coffee Company.** In this role, Mr. Ravener was responsible for the leadership and support of the people priorities and initiatives affecting more than 125,000 employees, across more than 10,000 company-operated and licensed stores. Prior to that assignment, Mr. Ravener served as Vice President, Partner Resources-Eastern Division.

Before joining Starbucks, Mr. Ravener served as Vice President, Human Resources for **The Home Depot**. During his tenure there, he held roles as both Vice President Human Resources for the Store Support Center and as Vice President Human Resources for one of three domestic divisions. In the latter role, Mr. Ravener was responsible for the Human Resources leadership of almost 700 stores and more than 100,000 employees in 23 states.

Prior to his position at The Home Depot, he was with **Footstar, Inc.**, the second largest footwear retailer in the US, serving for three years as Vice President, Chief Personnel Officer with a workforce of 22,000 and over 5,000 locations. He then moved into operations as a Senior Vice President, leading a multi-million business with over

2,000 employees. Mr. Ravener's retail experience also includes start-up operations, new business development, and acquisition integration.

Before Footstar, Mr. Ravener spent eleven years with **Pepsi-Cola** in positions of increasing responsibility in Human Resources, earning awards for leadership development and safety improvement. His experience at Pepsi included roles as a Senior Human Resource Generalist as well as benefits operations, safety and risk, and business re-engineering.

Mr. Ravener also served in the **US Navy** as a Strategic Weapons Submarine Officer aboard the USS *Daniel Webster* (SSBN 626), a fleet ballistic missile submarine. He was awarded the Navy Achievement Medal for his tour of duty. Mr. Ravener finished his active duty service at the US Naval Academy where he served as an instructor, coach, and recruiter. He also spent time in the Naval Reserves following active duty.

Mr. Ravener is a graduate of the **United States Naval Academy**, where he earned distinction as a leader, intercollegiate varsity baseball player, and is past president of his class. He also earned an MBA from **New York University**.

Mr. Ravener has been actively involved in service to the community through military veterans outreach, coaching of youth sports teams, Habitat for Humanity, and other volunteer efforts. He is a member of the Dollar General Literacy Foundation Board and has previously served on his community board for the Boys and Girls Club and the Ramapo College Board of Governors. In February of 2004, Mr. Ravener was appointed by the Secretary of Labor to the President's National Hire Veterans Committee and in 2007, was appointed to the

Secretary's Advisory Committee on Veterans Employment, Training, and Employer Outreach. In 2011 Mr. Ravener was also recognized in the Human Resources community as a Top 10 HR Breakaway Leader, in 2012 as a top HR executive by ExecRank, Inc., and under his leadership Dollar General has been nationally recognized for military support and training excellence.

Mr. Ravener resides in Brentwood, Tennessee, and is married with three children.

Contact him at bobravener.com.

Acknowledgments

Publishing this book has been a lengthy process, with the first pages being written in notes, articles, and photos depicting times in my life dating back to the 1960s. The more formal writing process began nearly twenty years ago and has been edited, rewritten, and compounded a great deal since that time.

None of what I have written in this book could have been accomplished without the help and partnership of many people. First and foremost is my family, who helped shape my life experiences and opinions over the years and has also been part of many of the events depicted in this story. So many of my relatives, friends, and colleagues also influenced my life—many of them mentioned in the preceding chapters. Neither can I forget all the great teachers and professors that molded my developing mind and challenged me to stretch my thinking to heights I never thought I could reach. I also have a special place in my heart for the US military and specifically the US Navy, which provided role models and shipmates, as well as training and experiential challenges. Without question, service in the military helped develop me beyond my wildest dreams.

Many thanks also go out to the people most responsible for bringing this book to print, a story that can best be told sequentially. In early 2009, literary professional Lola Honeybone and her husband, Andrew, were having dinner with my wife, Lisa, and me in Cool Springs, Tennessee, when the subject of my life story came up. Lola knew a literary agent and introduced me to Blythe Daniel, who thought my message had merit and signed on to represent me through The Blythe Daniel Agency. I vividly remember making that conference call—which included Blythe, Lola, and me—while my family and I were vacationing on the Outer Banks of North Carolina. Blythe spent the next three years aggressively, yet unsuccessfully, pitching the book to what seemed like countless publishing houses. They all rejected the project—not because of its content, they said, but because the industry was going through enormous change with the advent of Amazon, e-readers, and self-publishing. On top of that, I was an unknown author writing what many considered a memoir, and they just weren't interested.

Never one to give up, I was determined to get the book published, and Blythe recommended that I shorten the manuscript's length. She then introduced me to a freelance editor, Andrew Sloan, whom I hired to do the work. As we talked, I recognized that I was too close to the material to make an objective decision on what to eliminate or change. Andrew was a great help, and through many hours of editing back and forth, we ultimately were able to cut the content by a third. Shortly after we completed the edits, Blythe linked up with Eddie Jones at Lighthouse Publishing of the Carolinas, and he agreed to publish the book.

Eddie's able team and colleagues have also played an instrumental role in bringing the story to the public. Denise Loock spent many hours further refining and editing the book while Tim Burns and River Laker have partnered with me to get the additional elements of communicating, publicizing, and enhancing the book's message. Matt Hirsheimer, an amazing artistic talent, has offered some dazzling book cover ideas as his creative mind continues to produce great concepts.

I am deeply grateful to all those that have helped bring this book to life and will forever be indebted to them for their help and support.

Hall. A member of the audience, himself a pianist, came up to the artist after the concert. Briskly shaking the performer's hand, with much emotion he declared, "I would give anything to play like that!" The concert pianist looked the man square in the eye and replied, "No you wouldn't." Then he turned and walked away as the admirer stared in disbelief.

The concertgoer didn't appreciate that what he saw and heard was the result of years of training, countless hours of practice, and many struggles. The scenario is the same for virtually any exceptional achievement. Persevering through many years of sacrifice is undoubtedly a critical element to attaining any goal. Though I had a full-time job, a wife, and two young children, I went back to school after nine years. It meant going to classes two nights a week, year-round, for three and a half years. But I endured. My attitude helped me through that demanding phase of my life.

I've heard people complain about virtually everything. Whether it's a supervisor problem, a company's direction, family concerns—you name it—some people always take the low road. What's more, their negative attitude affects those around them, so before long there isn't just an individual issue but a broader team issue. Bad apples generally don't last long in organizations. They're too destructive to their environment and ultimately to themselves.

On the other hand, I have seen magical things happen to people with great attitudes. Almost invariably they are involved in more meetings, earn more trust from supervisors, and receive the best assignments and the promotions. Why? People like being around "positive waves." Just like negative waves impact others, positive ones do as well. And since people in general are drawn more quickly and closely to positive influences, individuals exhibiting those qualities are usually the first to move up the ladder. Any and all success I have enjoyed in life has been due, in large part, to attitude.

Reflection Questions

1. List a few people you really like to be around. Then list a few people you really *don't* like to be around. What common traits do the individuals in each category possess? How big of a part does attitude play?

2. Bob quotes Chuck Swindoll, who says that our attitude—the one thing we are in charge of—is more important than our education, money, circumstances, failures, successes, appearance, giftedness, or skill. How do you feel about those assertions?

3. In terms of the well-known idiom, do you generally see the glass as half full or half empty? Do you perceive the world to be full of problems or opportunities?

4. Bob shares how he has tried to encourage his son to exercise positive self-talk in the batter's box. How would you describe your self-talk?

5. Bob notes that certain types of reading and reflecting help him overcome the downward spiral of stewing over his own troubles. Has that kind of thing been helpful for you as well? If not, what does help you reverse that spiral?

6. Try the following exercise to foster a more positive attitude:

Divide a blank sheet of paper (or word-processing document) into a left and right column. On the left side, list all the positive things in your life, no matter how small or insignificant they seem. On the right side, list the negative things in your life—again, no matter how small or insignificant they seem.

As you evaluate the lists, you'll likely discover two things. First, there are more positive things in your life than you realized. Second, most of the negative things you listed are both manageable and, in the grand scheme of life, insignificant.

Here are the final two steps of this exercise: (1) Focus on the positive elements of your life by regularly reviewing that list and adding new entries. (2) Prioritize the negative elements. Try to remedy the situations that are easier to manage, thus gaining small wins that you can build on. As your attitude, energy, and confidence rise, devise ways to work on more items on the list.

Give Something Back

The highest reward for a person's toil is not what they get for it, but what they become by it.
~ John Ruskin

From the moment I began to receive accolades and attention, a metamorphosis took place within me. Caring only about myself, I became quite self-centered, convinced that I had endured enough hardship to deserve every good thing I received. Success bred more success, but it was one-sided. I was doing it all for me. And although the attention did help me fight my internal struggles, I felt empty, like there was really nothing to celebrate. I had already spent much of my life trying to prove my worth to the world, and nothing was going to prevent me from succeeding. I lived in a universe with one sun—me.

That line of reasoning, however, was doomed to failure. How could I continue to be so self-centered when every evening on the news I saw so much suffering throughout the world? In fact, all I had to do to see the strife of life spread out before my eyes was to take a wrong turn on my way to a game at Yankee Stadium and end up in the South Bronx. I couldn't erase those images, and at least I had enough humility to realize that "there but for the grace of God, go I."[5]

The challenge for me was learning how to view huge problems like world hunger without feeling compelled to

---

5   Attributed to John Bradford (1510-1555), English reformer and martyr

solve them. People often see pain they can't remedy, but their response is fleeting and frustrating because they feel powerless to do anything about it. I'm not just talking about donating to worthy causes. I have done that, but it still leaves an empty feeling because it may provide only a drop of water in a desert of misery.

Two things helped me realize that not only did I have something to give back to society, but that I had an obligation to do so. The first was the birth of my children, for whom I now had to be a role model. The second was remembering that I hadn't reached my level of success by myself, as much as I may have wanted to believe so. God was involved, as were the countless people who had nurtured, coached, and mentored me. The time had come for me to give back at least some of what I had been given.

A Music Lesson

Throughout my life, the lyrics of Harry Chapin's classic ballad, "Cat's in the Cradle," have influenced—maybe even haunted—me. The song tells the story of a father who constantly put off his young son's desire to spend time with him . . . until it was too late. The son grows up and doesn't have time for his dad. In the chorus, the son asks the dad when he's coming home, and the dad answers, "I don't know when, but we'll get together then. You know we'll have a good time then."[6]

I was determined not to be that dad.

When our oldest child, Cryssa, turned five, she became eligible to play soccer, her first team sport. As a member

---

6   Lyrics and Music by Harry Chapin. Album: *Verities and Balderdash*. 1974.

of just the second class at the Naval Academy to include females, I saw how they struggled in a former male-only fraternity. Later, I witnessed women's trials as they maneuvered through the male-dominated corporate world. Therefore, I was determined to shield my daughter from a similar fate.

The soccer league in Danbury, Connecticut, combined the boys and girls in order to field enough teams for a season. I volunteered to be an assistant coach, not because of my knowledge of the game (I hadn't played soccer since sixth grade) or because I was altruistic about my debt to society. No, it was much simpler than that. Since I was going to attend Cryssa's games anyway, why not help out? And as the assistant, I could always bail if I felt overextended or if complications arose. Besides, how could anyone expect me, with my busy schedule, to do any more than that?

It wasn't the first time I had volunteered. I had helped my brother-in-law when he coached his kids' Little League team. At that time, in my twenties, I couldn't see myself trying to teach kids who were only five or six years old how to play sports. The atmosphere had been completely social, not competitive. The instruction had been rudimentary— and, in reality, it didn't seem to make any difference. After playing at a competitive level all my life, I didn't think I had the patience to start over. Was I ever wrong!

My perspective was also completely off base. Coaching was likely the best way to ensure that I spent time with Cryssa. Once I made the commitment, I felt responsible to attend both practices and games. Up until then I hadn't worried about what time I left work; now I had another appointment, if you will, at the soccer field. Without even realizing it, I was scheduling time with my daughter.

Seeing the gleam in her eyes as we rushed around the house together, trying to get to practice on time, was truly rewarding. During practice, Cryssa often looked for me after she made a good kick to see if I had been watching. Then she smiled, as only a five-year-old can.

On top of that, watching the kids' transformation on the soccer field was nothing short of amazing. Between the first practice, when most of the kids didn't even know what the ball was for, and the end of the season, when they were actually passing the ball and working together as a team, their skills improved dramatically. Who would have thought that those fresh young faces, having received little structured teaching, would get it? But they did—and they thirsted for more.

Well, I was hooked. My parents had only attended a few of the activities in which I was involved. Remembering the pain caused by their absence, I wanted to be an integral part of my kids' lives.

The obstacle to that goal was "making a living." Breaking away from the office each day was difficult. I had plenty of work to do and too many meetings were scheduled for 5:00 p.m. I hadn't been the most confident guy all my life, so it wasn't easy for me to challenge the scheduling. I had struggled with the decision to be an "official" coach, but I also realized that being a coach required a deeper commitment to attend practices. Had I just been a casual observer, going to Cryssa's practices when it was convenient, chances are that I wouldn't have been there nearly as often. Actually, the need for an assistant coach opened a door for me to step up and fill the gap on her team.

After the soccer season that year, Cryssa played T-ball. Once again the teams were comprised of boys and girls who were five or six years old, and once again I volunteered as the assistant. Coaching a sport I knew something about, I needed to curb my ego and remember that many of the kids were seeing a baseball for the first time. They didn't disappoint us. On day one they didn't even know what the bases were, much less how to run them; however, they learned quickly, which led to a very successful season.

Coaching not only helped me avoid becoming the dad in "Cat's in the Cradle," it also taught me about child development. In soccer the boys dominated the girls, even at age five, so Cryssa didn't want to play soccer after that. The flow of play, basically, was student body left and then student body right, with all the kids chasing the ball regardless of position. As a result, the games became controlled chaos.

After we moved to Colorado, our younger daughter, Katie, was ready to take on soccer. Playing on an all-girl team made all the difference. Just three girls on each side and no goalie—a formula for success. Katie not only enjoyed the social aspects of the game, but in a much more tightly controlled environment she could also see and feel her progress. Cryssa, with all those players on the field, had been lucky to get a foot on the ball—much less score a goal. Katie, however, kicked the ball many times and also experienced the satisfaction of scoring goals. It's no wonder that Cryssa didn't want to play anymore, but Katie continued to play long after that first soccer season and eventually became a savvy, skillful force on the field.

My involvement with kids expanded to include soccer, baseball, basketball, and softball. While living in Colorado, I became a head coach. I agonized over the decision so much that when I originally sent in my registration, I volunteered to be an assistant. I was not only concerned about the time commitment, but I had also just been transferred and was beginning a new job in a new setting once again. My coaching status may have never changed if I hadn't received a phone call from the coordinator. He needed a head coach for a team of seven- to eight-year-olds. The rest is . . . well, you know.

Time Well Spent

Being a volunteer coach consumed countless hours of my time. Between that and working, doing anything for myself became almost impossible. But in the end it was worth it. By becoming a head coach, I accomplished two objectives. First, I spent quality time with my kids. And second, since I made up the practice schedule, I could factor in my work schedule and miss fewer events.

As all parents know, when kids reach school age the activities begin in earnest. The good news is that all kinds of activities are available to kids today (many more than when I attended school), which is good for their development but wreaks havoc on their parents—who have such a tough job already, juggling home life with work obligations like traveling to an out-of-town meeting or finishing a presentation. My wife, Lisa, was a great support too. She often brought snacks and helped with team logistics. She also cheered for the kids at every game.

Numerous justifiable responsibilities could have kept me away from my kids' events, but my life is so much fuller today because I chose to be intimately involved in their lives. Unlike my parents, I see my kids excel in their respective sports, and I never miss that special smile when they know I'm watching them. Though the scheduling of school-sponsored activities is beyond my control, I arrange my calendar so that I can attend as many events as possible.

Those who say their job prevents them from being involved in their children's lives need to rearrange their priorities. I have worked for companies like Pepsi-Cola, Home Depot, and Starbucks; currently, I work for Dollar General. Most experts consider these companies tough work environments in the sense that hard work, a fast pace, and long hours are part of the corporate landscape. But those companies have always supported my volunteer efforts, and all of them have been widely recognized for their community outreach. Without question, my tasks have to be completed, but I have squeezed a little bit more into my day and week to make it work. For me that has meant coming into the office earlier, working at home, or taking some time on weekends to fill the gaps. But I would rather do that than miss my kids growing up. Everyone has more control over their lives than they realize.

If I ever had any doubt about continuing to coach, I only needed to remember the letter I received after the 1996 softball season from the parents of one of the girls I coached:

Dear Bob:

Once upon a time there was a young man and a young lady.
They met in college, fell in love, and, after getting married,
had a beautiful little girl. The man and the lady thought the
little girl was the most wonderful child they had ever seen.
The little girl grew up and started reading nursery rhymes and
singing songs; the man and the lady thought it very darling to
hear her read.

One day, around her birthday, the little girl received a card in
the mail. She began to read the card aloud. This astonished
friends who were there visiting, as they had never seen a three-
year-old read so well. The man and the lady thought nothing
of it, for this was their darling little girl and everything she did
was wonderful and usual, since they had no other three-year-
old to compare her to.

Soon the little girl went to school, and by the time she had
half-completed the first grade the man and the lady were called
to school to discuss their daughter's academics. They were
surprised to find their first-grade daughter had been tested by a
specialist and was found to have the reading, writing, spelling,
and comprehension skills of an eighth-grader.

"What shall we do?" asked the teacher. "Do you want me to
take her out of class and treat her special?" The parents said,
"No, you treat her like any first-grader and we will treat her
special at home." The teacher was glad, as this was the response
she had hoped to hear from the man and the lady.

The man and the lady went home and made sure that the little girl had all the right books she needed. (That kept them busy since she loved to read and read and read.) Although the teacher agreed to treat the little girl like any other first-grader, her talents slowly began to appear to the other children and the other teachers. She was placed high on a pedestal by her peers. She knew she was on that pedestal and began to feel afraid of the height.

She began to withdraw, stopped playing, and eventually got an ulcer. When the man and the lady talked to the little girl, she confessed that she was terrified of getting an A– and wondered what would happen to her if she failed with an A–.

The man and the lady told her they loved her and they would be proud of anything she did as long as she *tried* her best. But nothing they could say would console their little girl. Each time she went to school she came home with perfect papers and a sadder heart.

Finally, one day the lady noticed that her little girl had the grace of a three-legged bovine. This gave the lady a very good idea. "We can *teach* our child to fail and she will see once and for all that it will be all right to come down from the pedestal." So the man and the lady put their little girl in softball.

The first year was hard on the little girl as she came tumbling down from her pedestal, but she always found her mom and dad cheering for her hard efforts. The little girl felt bruised by her fall, but soon learned that it wasn't such a bad fall after all; there were lots of friends at the bottom of the pedestal and lots of laughs and cheers. The little girl learned how to fail, to try, to fail, to try, and have fun trying and trying again. The lady and man kept telling her they were proud because she was trying hard and doing her best. "After all, Babe Ruth holds the record for strikeouts," they would tell her.

Now the little girl is in the fifth grade and still sits on an academic pedestal, but it is not so scary up there looking down, for now when she feels a falter in her strength she knows that the man and the lady will always be there for her to brush off the dust from the field and to encourage her to learn by failing and falling and to have fun while trying to climb back up.

Now the story could end here with this happy ending, but it doesn't. You see, the little girl kept playing softball, and she loved her coach, as he had as much patience with her *lack* of skill as a teacher has with her *excess* skill. She had a second season, which was better than the first, and then a third season, which was a "season to remember." Without even knowing it, the coach taught the little girl that she could tumble and fall, get hurt, try again, have fun, laugh, cry, and start all over again. And although she still has the grace of a three-legged bovine, the little girl has learned how to fail, and how to get back up on the pedestal.

Thank you very much for the lesson.

Sincerely yours,
The Man and the Lady

Parents don't often verbally affirm volunteers, but I know from casual conversations and the occasional letter that their efforts are deeply appreciated. And it's important for volunteer organizations to understand that a little gratitude of their own can go a long way.

All the volunteers I know are involved for basically three reasons, no different than my own. First, most of us volunteer because of our children. Every youth team I've coached has included one of my kids. Second, people volunteer because they have an affinity for helping or developing others. Something in a volunteer's makeup provides for the transfer of some knowledge they acquired through their own experience. One thing I enjoyed as a young human resources manager in Virginia was adopting a local grade school and having employees from the company speak to students about their jobs. It provided an enormous lift for the students since they could personalize the well-known Pepsi trademark. The employees received what I consider the third reason for volunteering: the satisfaction that comes from making a difference, however small, in someone's life.

Find Your Passion

But sports aren't my passion, you might be thinking. No matter what your passion is, volunteer opportunities exist for you to consider. Another passion of mine, which I have only realized in recent years, is serving veterans. Whether it's because of my family history, my firsthand appreciation for those who wear military uniforms, or the fact that the Navy contributed so much to my success in life, I have a profound inner passion for the armed forces. I cherished the opportunity to be a member of the President's National Hire Veterans Committee. As one of several representatives from corporate America and the government appointed by the Secretary of Labor, we were chartered to develop a strategy to promote the hiring of veterans in corporations. Few know that over two hundred thousand service members leave active duty each year, and that the work force includes over fifty thousand military spouses and over twelve million veterans (of the approximately twenty-three million still living). My involvement in the committee has done more for me than I could ever do to help our veterans, but hopefully my effort has contributed in some small way.

In 2012, colleagues of mine at Dollar General and I partnered with the state of Tennessee's Departments of Labor, Veterans Affairs, and National Guard to create the "Paychecks for Patriots" initiative, which brought together almost 100 employers across the state in a single day to promote the hiring of military veterans and their spouses in thirteen separate locations. The concept is now spreading to other states, and it is the best example I have seen in my career of the public and private sectors working together for a common cause. Efforts like this help me remember that all things are possible.

I have been involved in volunteer work since my childhood. As a Cub Scout in grade school, I often volunteered for the various civic activities the school held in the community. That carried over into high school, where I was involved in student council, yearbook staff, ring and prom committees, and more. I was president of my Naval Academy class and have been responsible for subsequent class reunions. Since graduating from the Academy, I have been involved in political campaigns, and among other things, started the alumni association for my high school, taught Sunday school, served on the board of directors of the local Boys and Girls Club, and sat on several senators' service academy selection boards in three different states.

I don't mention my volunteer services to boast. I am merely suggesting that others have both the capability and opportunity to volunteer as well. I have never expected anything more than to see my efforts achieve the desired goal, whether that is developing kids, getting someone elected, or creating a cleaner environment. For me, just receiving a personal note of thanks made specific volunteer efforts worthwhile. Nobody has ever had to beg me to do something again when I felt it was appreciated.

An Urgent Need

I am but one that has broken the cycle among millions subjected to the challenges related to substance abuse, domestic violence, and poverty. That cycle continues for many people, and it must be addressed if our nation is to continue to prosper. The overall state of well-being among the disenfranchised doesn't seem to improve. Census data through 2011 indicated that nearly fifty million Americans live below the poverty line, the highest level over the fifty-one years since poverty estimates have been available. That number includes almost 20 percent of American children, despite the vast sums of money poured into programs designed to remove this societal ball and chain.

Poverty fuels other challenges: stunted learning and literacy, sub-standard living and health, crime, substance abuse, and violence—just a few of the more dire consequences. More than sixteen million alcohol dependent citizens or those who have problems with alcohol live in the United States. Illicit drug use (not including marijuana) has stricken another twenty million people according to the National Institute on Drug Abuse. The destructive impact of those affected by substance abusers is immeasurable. Functional illiteracy plagues over forty million American adults according to The National Right to Read Foundation. The Domestic Violence Resource Center estimates that up to twelve million men, women, and children are subject to violence at home. The vast majority of the pain is inflicted on women and the children that witness the abuse.

What should be done? First, individuals need to take personal responsibility for their lives and think hard about the choices they make every day. Nothing was handed to me, although many people helped me along the way. I was a product of our public school system and was blessed with caring teachers, but I chose to open my mind and allow them to assist me. I also found solace and hope in those who helped propel my drive and determination to climb out of the hole of despair. And I didn't want to disappoint those who supported me.

Another crucial factor in my growth and healing was learning to confide in others. I never even talked about my circumstances until Lisa became my confidante, early in our marriage. She helped me put the pieces of the puzzle together. I had kept all that strife and grief bottled up well into my twenties. She provided a sounding board and allowed me to express my feelings. But how many people never open up to anyone?

By making a positive difference in my life, I was then able to make a difference in the lives of others. So much help is needed across a multitude of organizations that all you need to do, in most cases, is ask if you can help. When I first volunteered to coach, I stated up front that I would have some conflicts, which was never a problem since I always had a capable assistant coach to cover for me. That opened the door for me to get involved. Since then, I have been involved in one way or another with many other worthwhile causes. They all need volunteer support to complete their missions. Your local community probably has a homeless shelter, a soup kitchen, Boys and Girls Clubs, Habitat for Humanity, or any number of other worthy organizations that need help. So find your voice. Be a part of the solution.

Initially, my reward was spending time with my kids and forging memories that neither they nor I will ever forget. I then realized that helping people through volunteer work generated many other rewards. Throughout my life, including my military career, the organizations with which I've been associated have had some service component as part of their operational structure. Your church, workplace, or community most likely does too. Just look around, find something that interests you, and then ask, "What can I do to help?"

My final encouragement about giving is this: whatever you do, never look for something in return. To me, that is the true definition of giving.

Reflection Questions

1. How much were you involved in volunteer work through your school, church, or community when you were growing up?

2. Much of this chapter focuses on Bob's experience as a volunteer coach for his children's sports teams. What motivates you to volunteer? What have been your most rewarding situations as a volunteer? Have you had any negative experiences?

3. How do you feel about your ability to balance work, doing things for yourself, and giving to others? How do you feel about Bob challenging those who say their job prevents them from being a volunteer to get their priorities in order?

4. How much affirmation or appreciation have you received for your volunteer efforts? How has that affected your motivation to continue serving?

5. How could you tap into something you are passionate about in a way that would make a difference in the lives of others?

6. Think of something natural or convenient that you could plug into as a volunteer, such as your church or your child's school or sports team. Whatever the endeavor, take a step forward and get involved.

Values Define You

When what we want to do and what we ought to do are two different things, character is built in the choice we make.
~Bill Bennett

On March 12, 2009, Bernie Madoff pled guilty to what is widely considered the largest individual fraud case in US history. Madoff swindled thousands of people out of nearly $65 billion through a Ponzi scheme that he masterminded for several decades. Major league baseball has been forever tarnished by the steroids scandal that has plagued the sport in recent years, clouding the accomplishments of many stars that have disgraced "America's Pastime."

Unethical behavior also runs rampant elsewhere in society. The American people don't trust their elected officials in Washington because scandal after scandal riddles the halls of Congress and the White House. Corporations have come under tremendous scrutiny due to the misdeeds of the executives in companies like Enron, Tyco, and others. On April 4, 1997, a *USA Today* headline read, "Doing the Wrong Thing: 48 Percent of Workers Admit to Unethical or Illegal Acts." Examples from the article, which conveyed an alarming increase in theft and fraud in the workplace, included the following: Prudential ordered to pay $1 billion to policyholders who were bilked into buying more expensive life insurance than they needed, executives from Archer Daniels Midland on trial for price fixing, and Texaco employees accused of discrimination.

I vividly recall taking a nickel off the kitchen counter when I was seven years old so I could buy candy on the way to school. What I remember most is how guilty I felt all day. The nickel didn't belong to me, and my conscience couldn't ignore that breach of trust. Even when I bought a pack of Mint Juleps—a kid-favored assortment of individually wrapped chewy taffy—my heart felt sick. After school, I was torn between telling my mother and risking punishment or maintaining my silence and risking relentless obsession with my crime. One thing was clear: the longer I held on to my secret, the worse I felt. Finally, with tears streaming down my face, I told my mother everything. Much to my surprise—and relief—she didn't punish me. Instead, she told me that God was watching me and that stealing nickels could lead to actions that would land me in jail. That was one of the few times I remember receiving valuable words of wisdom from either of my parents.

Since then, every time I have done something even a little off-center, guilt has welled up inside me. Like most kids, I disobeyed my parents, skipped a class or two, and drove too fast after getting my license. Sometimes I faltered, but people often said that I had a good head on my shoulders, which translates into good judgment. And after years of trial and error, I've learned that discernment is really quite simple: if you're about to do something that doesn't feel 100 percent okay, either don't do it or be prepared to feel that empty pit in your stomach when you do.

Honorable Intentions

Positive values not only define the good in a person but also define who that person is. Here is my list of core values:

- honesty/integrity

- morality

- commitment

- courage

- tenacity

- loyalty

- accountability

- trust in God

Without these core values, life has no meaning. They are the foundation of my existence. Unfortunately, the values I strive to live by now weren't instilled in me as a child. More unfortunate is the fact that many people never learn and practice critical values, which has precipitated the demise of many families and communities.

In my case, people who had these core values entered my life and I learned from their examples. My first lessons came at the Naval Academy. From day one, midshipmen are taught that integrity is paramount not only to good order and discipline but also to survival itself. The honor concept at Navy, similar to that of the other military academies, states that a midshipman will not lie, cheat, or steal. The codes at Army and Air Force take it a step further by stating that a cadet will not tolerate anyone else that lies, cheats, or steals. Honor is critical on the field of battle. It is also critical on the job and in everyday life. When trust exists, good things happen. When trust is absent, it's much harder to accomplish anything worthwhile.

When I was in high school and college, my sense

of right and wrong was sometimes skewed. Although I
always thought I had a good head and a good heart, I
believed that a good time meant drinking with my buddies
and chasing girls. Academically, I did what I considered
necessary to excel, but I don't think I reached my full
potential until some years later. Why? In a small town
without much to do, young people typically try to stir
up some excitement. As a result, a "good" Friday night
consisted of jumping in someone's car, going to a liquor
store we knew wouldn't ask for identification, and buying a
few six-packs for the road. Then we would either look for a
party or stop and drink before heading to a local club that,
again, was lax on IDs.

Even though my friends and I were under the legal
drinking age of eighteen, we were too naïve to care. In
retrospect, I don't know how many times my life or
someone else's was endangered because of teenage drinking.
And in light of how much effort it takes to succeed at work
and at home, many people don't realize how much time is
lost because of a "good night out," especially on a school or
work night.

When I was sixteen, I worked at the local diner. I was
doing well in school and excelling in sports. I also had a
girlfriend. Life doesn't get much better for a sixteen-year-
old. Dave Donigian, who owned the diner and always had
a smile on his face, was an excellent boss and mentor for
me. I started out bussing tables and eventually worked my
way up to short-order cook. Performing multiple tasks and
trying to please customers, some of whom weren't easy to
please, was certainly a growth experience for me. All in all I
had a great setup. So good, in fact, that after school started
in the fall, Dave kept me on during the week to open up
at 6:00 a.m. before school and to come back after my last

sports practice of the day to clean up. Balancing everything going on in my life required the precision of a circus performer. I had to be as organized and focused as possible. Disappointing Dave wasn't an option.

Lessons Learned

But I did let him down. One night after a basketball game, a tough loss, some of my friends were going out for a few beers and I decided to join them. Unfortunately, as is often the case, a few beers led to a few more, and so on, until it became quite late. I never made it to the diner to clean up. And because I came home a little inebriated, I forgot to set my alarm clock.

I was sound asleep when the phone rang at 6:00 a.m. It was Dave. He was angry about the condition in which he found the diner and even more irate about the fact that I didn't open up the restaurant that morning. Luckily, Dave had come in early, but the displeasure in his voice jolted me awake.

I rushed to get dressed and raced to the diner. As usual, the place was packed with customers. I immediately went into the backroom and began the cleanup process, which by now entailed twice as much work because of the breakfast dishes. Dave didn't say another word about it to me, but his face betrayed his disappointment. Nothing I could say would change that look, but I knew that I could never let it happen again.

That sequence of events taught me an extremely valuable lesson about being responsible, one that helped frame my future. Dave could have rationalized that he had been working me too hard or that since he was already there he could just clean up the diner himself. Or he could have fired me. Instead, he cared enough about me and about the responsibility he had given me to address the situation immediately and directly. Many people won't do that, which is a disservice to those to whom they are giving responsibility.

The experience also taught me that responsibility comes before pleasure, and I never again let alcohol or a good time prevent me from completing my committed responsibilities. In fact, I rarely drink anymore, and when I do, it is in moderation. Life is too short!

Today, when I question the value of something I'm about to do, I ask myself what the payoff is and what I would tell my children to do in the same instance. Some wise person said that we can do ninety-nine positive things but one breech of integrity can ruin all the good we've done. Therefore, I do the right thing because it's the right thing to do. I don't preach my values to others, but I certainly try to live by them.

Risking Tragedy

Throughout this book I have mentioned numerous people who have impacted my life. Everyone is influenced by others. Some interactions, such as with parents and other family members, are unavoidable. And you may be unable to do anything about being assigned a particular teacher or boss. In many situations, however, you control whom you associate with, listen to, and basically build your life around. Though you may not choose your teammates on the field, you control which players you hang out with off the field. Your latitude is infinitely greater when it comes to your friends.

Even in circumstances that are unfavorable, you can control much of how they affect you. Let's say, for instance, that you have a parent or sibling who uses drugs and breaks the law. You can choose to engage in the same type of behavior, or you can move in another direction. If you have a lousy boss, you can try to work through the situation, or you can find a better situation.

When I was young, I followed everyone else because I wanted to belong and to be liked. I was a classic follower. That trait propelled me into a couple of situations that could have ended up scarring me for a long time.

For example, one day when I was eight or nine, a friend, Guy, and I were walking home after a Little League baseball game along a road near a highway overpass. Guy thought it would be "cool" to drop a stone off the overpass wall and see what would happen. Though I wasn't thinking of the potential injury or even death that could have occurred, the idea still seemed wrong. Yet Guy persisted, calling me several names because I was reluctant to join him. Since he was my closest friend and I was afraid he would reject me, I took the penny-sized stone he handed me even though I still wasn't willing to toss it. At that point I knew Guy was a little nervous too: he paced back and forth across the overpass several times while he kept daring me. I said I wasn't going to throw mine first, but I would if he did. Doesn't that sound like a classic kids' confrontation?

After several minutes, Guy tossed his stone over the side of the wall, and we watched the speeding traffic below to see what would happen. Instantly, a car screeched its brakes, pulled off the road, and began to back up on the shoulder. We could see that the passenger's side of the windshield had been shattered, and we could tell that the car was heading for the off-ramp. I dropped my stone over the side of the overpass so I could say I did it too, and we both took off in a sprint to make our getaway.

Before we fled from the scene of the crime, I glanced over the side of the wall. Apparently, my stone hadn't hit a car, but that didn't matter. I had been involved and was just as guilty as Guy. We quickly came to a side street and ran behind a store to hide out. My heart was pounding both from running and from the thought of being caught. Although my mind was whirling, time seemed to stand still. I just wanted the incident to end or for the stones to be back in our hands.

After waiting for what seemed like forever, though I'm sure it was only ten or fifteen minutes, we emerged from our hiding place, thinking that we must have ditched the car. No sooner had we resumed our journey home, however, than a car stopped alongside the street curb and a big man jumped out. With fire in his eyes he screamed, "Stop right there! You thought you could get away from me, didn't you?!" He continued shouting at us while gesturing toward the car. We knew he was driving the car the stone hit because there was not only a hole in the windshield—which had cracked from end to end—but the stone was also lying on the dashboard. The man said, "Once I saw your ball caps on the overpass, it wasn't hard to spot you again." At that point I reached up, touched my ball cap, and realized that I certainly wasn't cut out to be a criminal.

Guy and I initially tried to run, but the man grabbed both of us by the arms. His grip was like a vice, so my guilt turned to stark terror because I was unsure what that hulk of a man was going to do to us. As we squirmed in an effort to free ourselves from his lock, he said he had lost us once and wasn't going to let that happen again. Holding both of us with one massive hand, he pulled out an ID and said he was a truant officer, had the right to arrest us, and could haul us to the police station. For all I knew he had showed us a Rotary Club membership card, but I was too frightened to challenge him. We begged him to let us go, but he pushed us into the backseat of his car and drove off. Imagine our terror—two Little Leaguers in the backseat of a beat-up car, the driver as mad as hell and all his anger directed toward us.

Not knowing what to think, I asked the man where he was taking us. After a long pause, he said, "Tell me where you live." Now going to the police was one thing, but having to face my parents was quite another. Guy and I looked at each other, stayed silent for a painful moment, and gulped. I didn't know what was worse: being in the car with a stranger who could dump us on the side of the road or knowing that he was taking us either to the police or to our parents.

We finally told the man where we lived, and he took off in that direction. After driving for what seemed like an eternity, he stopped at Guy's house. Nobody was home (obviously not my day). Next he drove to my house, which was only a block away. Ordering us to get out of the car, he then followed us to the front door. Once inside, he ranted about our delinquency and demanded to be paid for the damage. My father may have been a drunk, but he was no dummy. He and my mother both told the guy to call his insurance company and send them a bill for any out-of-pocket deductible.

When he finally left, growling under his breath about the state of youth, my parents turned toward me and grounded me for the rest of my life. No, actually they punished me for the incident but then shared some real wisdom about where acts like that would lead. The other advice my parents gave me was to stay away from Guy. It wasn't the first time he had lured me into mischief, and they knew it.

From that point on I kept my distance from Guy, and to this day I'm relieved that nobody was seriously hurt because of our senseless act. The stone could have hit the driver's side of the windshield, caused him to lose control and crash into other vehicles and injured or even killed the man or other people. And after being tossed in the car of a total stranger, we were fortunate that he didn't drive to some remote location and molest us, or worse.

I was lucky that day, but I also learned two valuable lessons. First, choose friends wisely. Second, be my own person, strong and ethical, in marginal circumstances. In other words, do the right thing no matter what. That lesson wasn't lost on me. From that day forward, I chose friends who worked hard. They were also good role models and citizens. And while I went out of my way to be cordial, I stayed an arm's distance away from those who were misdirected.

I've had lapses of good judgment, but with determination to stay on course, my errors were eventually correctable. Numerous opportunities have arisen throughout my life where I could have moved in the wrong direction, but with God's help I have associated with some exceptional people. I owe a great deal to them. Countless people have helped mold me into who I am today. Every one of them has touched my life, changing it forever. My close friends and associates have commanded US Navy ships, submarines, and squadrons. Others are top human resources executives at major companies. Still others are running major businesses and other organizations.

People impact you. If you associate with good people, good things will come of it. If you don't, less than desirable outcomes are likely. Values transcend people and actions.

Reflection Questions

1. Who has been a model of integrity in your life?

2. Bob recounts three youthful incidents of bad judgment (stealing a nickel, letting his boss down, and tossing a stone from an overpass). Does that spark some memories from your younger days? What role did your conscience play in your story/stories? What role does your conscience play in your life and decision-making now?

3. What values are on your short list of critical core values? What individuals and experiences have contributed to the process of establishing your core values?

4. What do you think of Bob's point that we choose our friends? You might enjoy spending time with your friends, but are they making you a better person?

5. Do you have any friends that you need to consider backing away from? What steps could you take to develop better friendships?

6. Do you have any relationships that are both unhealthy and unavoidable with a family member or boss? If so, what is the best way for you to control how that relationship affects you?

Living in the Zone

Success demands singleness of purpose.
~ Vince Lombardi

In terms of a focused effort, perhaps no feat in history has been better chronicled or more celebrated than the race to the moon. Although the United States and the Soviet Union had been involved in space programs since the 1940s, what really catapulted America forward was President John F. Kennedy's speech to a special joint session of Congress on May 25, 1961, in which he issued this challenge: "I believe that this nation should commit itself to achieving the goal, before this decade is out, of landing a man on the moon and returning him safely to earth."

At the time, the United States lagged behind the Soviets in the space race, but Kennedy's words spurred NASA into action. On January 27, 1967, NASA suffered the tragic setback of three astronauts' deaths in Apollo 1. Nevertheless, just two and one-half years later, on July 20, 1969, Neil Armstrong, commander of Apollo 11, stepped onto the moon's surface, a feat the Soviets never achieved. The moon landing is a tremendous example of how a focused approach can achieve what many claimed was unattainable. In just eight years, a dream of historic and long-lasting proportions was realized, and the nation was energized in the process.

Clear Your Head

People often ask me how I can be involved in so many activities without imploding. My response is always the same: I have learned, over years of trial and error, what I am capable of doing. I have also discovered that when my head is clear of distractions and focused on the specific task at hand, I am successful in that endeavor. However, when my mind is cluttered with scattered thoughts, I become unfocused and unable to accomplish my task or, at the very least, I am unable to do my best.

For example, during my final season as a high school baseball player, I struggled with a cluttered mind. The previous year I had hit .494 on our 14–6 team. Therefore, as a senior co-captain, I was looking for the crowning finish to my high school career by improving that average. Our team was also picked to win our conference. So right away I put pressure on myself. In the first regular season game I went hitless in four at-bats, and after the first four games I was batting just .250. I began to think something was wrong with my swing or my stance.

Then our assistant coach, John Wrenn, an outstanding athlete, pulled me aside one day. When he told me that I was pressing too hard, I realized the problem was in my head. I had hit a slump, as virtually every athlete does at some point. Coach Wrenn encouraged me to relax at the plate and not worry about hits. He also bluntly told me to stop worrying about my own statistics and focus on how I could help the team. His advice was simple: help the team in other ways until the hits come. As the number-two pitcher on the team, I focused on that part of the game. I also took my duty as a captain more seriously. After all, I was supposed to be a leader and help my teammates.

Within a few games, the slump evaporated and the hits multiplied. Our team finished with a 16–2 record and won the school's first team championship. My batting average for the season was .455, and I was named to Connecticut's high school all-star team. All that success was generated by changing what was in my head, not in my swing. The lesson for me? The clearer my mind, the more I can accomplish.

Most people point to the adage that "there are only so many hours in a day" as proof that they can't accomplish a great deal and have a great quality of life as well. I used to feel that way, too, until I realized that individuals who are in more demanding positions than I can get a whole lot done. Just look at the President of the United States, the CEO of a major company—or a working mother, for that matter. They must complete many tasks every day, but they have no more hours in a day than anybody else. How do they do it? Their secret is that they know, better than others, *how* to get things done. And what is most evident is their ability to delegate some duties to others. You might argue that some people, like the President, have unlimited resources at their disposal, but so do many others who may accomplish very little.

A Good Game Plan Improves Productivity and Success

The wise use of time is a learned skill. From the day I arrived at the Naval Academy, the demands on my time were fierce. I learned quickly that if I was going to survive and graduate I had to adapt to the following weekday schedule:

Midshipman Daily Schedule

5:30 a.m.	Reveille/fitness training
6:30	Plebe instruction period
7:00	Morning meal formation/breakfast
7:55	Morning classes begin (four periods)
11:45	Classes end
12:05 p.m.	Noon meal formation/lunch
12:40	Company training time
1:30	Afternoon classes begin
3:30	Classes end/athletic activities begin
6:30	Evening meal formation/dinner
7:30	Study time begins
11:00	Lights out for plebes
Midnight	Taps for upperclassmen

In the fleet, the demands increased even more. During a typical day at sea, I stood watch in the control room from midnight to six o'clock while most of the rest of the ship's officers were sleeping. From about seven o'clock until noon we did various drills like flooding, fires, or battle stations. Then I had three divisions—torpedo, fire control, and sonar—to lead, which consisted of about thirty sailors. Finally, I took time to sleep, usually less than six hours a day.

When I joined Pepsi after serving in the Navy, a whole new set of expectations and demands were placed on my time. My responsibilities included conducting contract negotiations, handling employee disputes, recruiting, facilitating training classes, and answering on average forty voice mails a day. Promotions always come with new

Made in the USA
Lexington, KY
14 May 2014